NONCONFORMITY

WRITING ON WRITING

NELSON ALGREN

AFTERWORD BY DANIEL SIMON

NOTES BY
DANIEL SIMON AND C. S. O'BRIEN

SEVEN STORIES PRESS • NEW YORK

A Seven Stories First Edition
All rights reserved

Copyright © 1996 by The Estate of Nelson Algren
Afterword copyright 1996 © by Daniel M. Simon
Printed in the United States of America

Library of Congress Cataloging-in-Publication Data
Algren, Nelson, 1909-
Nonconformity : writing on writing / by Nelson Algren : edited and
with an afterword by Daniel Simon.
        p.   cm.
ISBN 1-888363-05-3
1. Algren, Nelson, 1909-   —Authorship. 2. Authorship—Political
aspects—United States—History—20th century. 3. Novelists, American—
20th century—Biography. I. Simon, Daniel, 1957-   .
II. Title.
PS3501.L46257465   1996
813'.52—dc20
[8]
                                94-35205
CIP
10 9 8 7 6 5 4 3 2 1
        Interior designed by Martin Moskof

CONTENTS

Nonconformity 1

I. 3

II. 9

III. 17

IV. 25

V. 33

VI. 45

VII. 55

VIII. 65

IX. 73

Afterword 81
    Historical Note and
    Acknowledgements 98

Appendix 113

Notes 121

Q: *What is sentimentality? What is sentimental?*

Algren: Oh, it's an indulgence in emotion. You want men and women to be good to each other and you're very stubborn in thinking that they want to be. Sentimentality is a kind of indulgence in this hope. I'm not against sentimentality. I think you need it. I mean, I don't think you get a true picture of people without it in writing.

Q: Go on.

Algren: It's a kind of poetry, it's an emotional poetry, and, to bring it back to the literary scene, I don't think anything is true that doesn't have it, that doesn't have poetry in it.

—H. E. F. Donohue
from *Conversations with Nelson Algren*
1963

NONCONFORMITY

I.

THE STRUGGLE TO WRITE WITH PRO-
fundity of emotion and at the same time to live
like a millionaire so exhausted F. Scott
Fitzgerald that he was at last brought down to
the point where he could no longer be both a
good writer and a decent person.

"So... I would cease any attempts to be a person—
to be kind, just or generous," he planned. "I felt like the
beady-eyed men I used to see on the commuting train...,
men who didn't care whether the world tumbled into chaos
tomorrow if it spared their houses..., who said: 'I'm sorry
but business is business.' Or: 'You ought to have thought of
that before you got into this trouble.' Or: 'I'm not the person to see about that....'

"This is what I think now," Fitzgerald continued:
"that the natural state of the sentient adult is a qualified
unhappiness. I think also that in an adult the desire to be
finer in grain than you are... only adds to this unhappiness
in the end...."[1]

An observation so melancholy as to recall Mark

Twain, after one of his last lectures, turning to a friend to say, "Oh, Cable, I am demeaning myself. I am allowing myself to be a mere buffoon. It's ghastly. I can't endure it any longer."[2]

The writer's lot, like the policeman's, is never a happy one. A hardy life, as the poet says, with a boot as quick as a fiver. But it isn't till now, in the American Century as we have recklessly dubbed it, that tribal pressures toward conformity have been brought to bear so ruthlessly upon men and women seeking to work creatively.

"Our tragedy today is a general and universal physical fear so long sustained by now that we can even bear it," William Faulkner puts it. "There are no longer problems of the spirit. There is only the question: when will I be blown up? Because of this, the young man or woman writing today has forgotten the problems of the human heart in conflict with itself which alone can make good writing...."[3]

I purely doubt that the young man or woman writing today has forgotten the problems of the heart in conflict with itself. I doubt he's forgotten a thing. And knows as well as any man that he labors under a curse. But how can a young unknown be expected to risk that consultation of the heart from which the older hands flee? The spectacle of artists like Elia Kazan, Jose Ferrer and Maxwell Anderson[4] leaping through the hoop at the first sight of the whip doesn't encourage the younger man to hold his ground. He knows enough of the heart to know it cannot conform. He knows there is no Feinberg Law and no Broyles bills[5] for the heart; that the heart's only country is the earth of Man.

But what, when Howard Hughes discovers that somebody on the payroll once belonged to ADA,[6] will the accused be able to say in self-defense? Whether he's in writing, TV, radio, teaching or lecturing, he sees very well, the way things are going, that the main thing is not problems of the heart, but to keep one's nose clean. Not to trouble oneself about the uneasy hearts of men. But to pass, safe and dry-shod, down the rushing stream of time.[7]

Between the pretense and the piety of American business in praising peace everywhere while preferring profits in warplanes anywhere, between the H Bomb and the A, the young man or woman whom you remind of the eternal verities this morning will only reply, "You ought to have thought of that before you got into this trouble."

Our tragedy today is a general and universal physical fear so long sustained by now that we can even bear it. There are no longer problems of the spirit. There is only the question: when will I be blown up? Because of this, the young man or woman writing today has forgotten the problems of the human heart in conflict with itself which alone can make good writing because only that is worth writing about, worth the agony and the sweat.

He must learn them again. He must teach himself that the basest of all things is to be afraid; and, teaching himself that, forget it forever, leaving no room in his workshop for anything but the old verities and truths of the heart, the old universal truths lacking which any story is ephemeral and doomed—love and honor and pity and pride and compassion and sacrifice. Until he does so, he labors under a curse. He writes not of love but of lust, of defeats in which nobody loses anything of value, of victories without hope and, worst of all, without pity or compassion. His griefs grieve on no universal bones, leaving no scars. He writes not of the heart but of the glands.

Until he relearns these things, he will write as though he

stood among and watched the end of man. I decline to accept the
end of man. It is easy enough to say that man is immortal simply
because he will endure: that when the last ding-dong of doom has
clanged and faded from the last worthless rock hanging tideless in
the last red and dying evening, that even then there will still be
one more sound: that of his puny inexhaustible voice, still talking.
I refuse to accept this. I believe that man will not merely endure:
he will prevail. He is immortal, not because he alone among crea-
tures has an inexhaustible voice, but because he has a soul, a spirit
capable of compassion and sacrifice and endurance. The poet's, the
writer's, duty is to write about these things. It is his privilege to
help man endure by lifting his heart, by reminding him of the
courage and honor and hope and pride and compassion and pity
and sacrifice which have been the glory of his past. The poet's
voice need not merely be the record of man, it can be one of the
props, the pillars to help him endure and prevail.

—William Faulkner,
Address upon receiving the Nobel Prize for Literature,
Stockholm, December 10, 1950[8]

II.

"IF YE'D TURN ON TH' GAS IN TH' DARKEST heart," Mr. Dooley liked to say, "ye'd find it had a good raison for th' worst things it done, a good varchous[9] raison like needin' th' money or punishin' th' wicked or tachin' people a lesson to be more careful, or protectin' th' liberties iv mankind, or needin' th' money."[10]

If you turn up the gas in the hearts of our business brass you'll find a good reason—a good varchous reason—for investing more and more heavily in the Korean adventure. Such as protecting the liberties of mankind. Or needing the money. Just as the Russians employ various alarms—Trotskyism, Zionism, counter-revolution—to divert criticism, so do our air force magnates use the bogey of Communism to keep the war-orders mounting.

Charles E. Wilson, writing in the *Army Ordnance Journal* as far back as 1944, feels we ought to be less secretive about such orders: "War has been inevitable in our human affairs as an evolutionary force.... Let us make the three-way partnership (industry, government, army) permanent." "Those nations that profess to fear our methods most will soon be most closely imitating those methods," was how Adolf Hitler put it. And echo answers: "What is good for General Motors is good for the country." "So soon as you have a military class," Woodrow Wilson agreed with Mr. Dooley, "elections are of minor importance."

Five years have passed since we began, once again, to rearm. Do we therefore feel more free from attack than we did five years ago? Have we thereby established an abiding trust in the hearts of other peoples? Do we therefore find ourselves with more friends in the world? Are our rights as free men thus made more secure? Or have we not once more demonstrated that keeping industries that depend for profit upon war and the preparation of war (such as the aviation industry) in private hands is equivalent to putting a hot-car thief in charge of a parking lot?

So it must be that, in the present senatorial passion for investigation, the reason nobody investigates the men who are trading off our freedoms for private enrichment is that they are the very ones who are doing the investigating. The Senate Subcommittee on Privileges and Elections, reporting on Joe McCarthy's bilking of Lustron and Seaboard Airlines,[11] and his manipulation in futures, announced that "this is a matter that transcends partisan politics and goes into the very core of the Senate body's authority and the respect in which it is held by the people of the country." Yet not a single senator protested when the worst con man to be elected to the United States Senate took his seat. Not a single one dared. "They know by this time they cannot turn me aside," McCarthy explained—and for the first time he spoke the truth. Between the pretense and the piety. Between the H Bomb and the A.

Say I'm standing knee-deep, and sinking, in the muddy waters of the Little Calumet. Some anxious-looking patriot paddles up, identifying himself as the Washington correspondent of *The New Yorker* bringing men tidings of comfort and joy: namely, that if the Little Calumet were the Volga I'd be up to my ears. And paddles away as contentedly as if he'd really done something for me.

He hasn't done a thing, this roving mercenary with the shaky gerund. Not even when he warns me that I better stop saying *Ouch* when McCarthy gives the screw another turn—lest the Kremlin overhear my yip and tape-record it for rebroadcasting to Europe. Who's paying *him* for God's sake?

The insistence of these long-remaindered intellectuals on the short leashes that, compared to the drive for conformity in the USSR, we don't have any notion as yet of what the real thing can be like, reveals loyalty to nobody save Henry Luce. Whose dangerous dictum it is that it is now America's part "to exert upon the world the full impact of our influence for such purposes as we see fit and by such means as we see fit."

"America does not go abroad," John Quincy

Adams corrects him, "in search of monsters to destroy."
Monsters enough roam in the woods at home. And watching Luce and McCarthy battle is like watching a couple of
dinosaurs go at it—it doesn't make any difference which
wins, because they're both extinct.

If they're not, then we are. The great confident
majority of Americans Adlai Stevenson described as "the generous and the unfrightened, those who are proud of our
strength and sure of our goodness and who want to work
with each other in trust, to advance the honor of the country." If they're not extinct, then the philosophy of strength
through freedom of speech is being replaced, Justice Douglas
warns, by the philosophy of strength through repression.

No people to date has obtained a corner on Truth.
And when we elect a pair of ragged claws to the Senate of
the United States we forfeit something of our own claim. It
no longer suffices to doubt such war heroes privately. The
out-loud kind of doubting that rescued American thought,
in the twenties, from the files where the McCarthys and
McCarrans[12] and Jenners of that decade had locked it, is
what is most needful to the States in the fifties. For Dreiser
and Mencken, Sinclair Lewis and Veblen and Steffens and
all, all are down in the dust of the twenties.[13]

And once again the little editorial fellows in the
London collars, and the underwear unchanged for weeks,
are hawking the alarm on every newsstand that only by
napalm and thunder-jet may the American way of life be

saved. That no man may now call himself loyal who will not pledge allegiance to the commander of the closest American Legion Post and to that mob-mindedness for which he stands.[14] That by placing economic boycotts on dissenters we thereby ensure the liberties of conformists. That what is good for Jake Margarine is good for the country. That by hobbling our scientists and teachers we guarantee academic freedom. That if we can but build a space platform before anyone else we shall thus ensure national contentment for keeps. And that in its capacity to wage technological warfare across another people's soil lies proof enough of any nation's greatness. Babbitt has risen from the dust of the twenties, his fingers fit the levers of power and the lid is off on the price of nonconformity.

"Before long," Mark Twain wrote, "you will see this curious thing: the speakers stoned from the platform and free speech strangled by hordes of furious men who in their secret hearts are still at one with these stoned speakers—but do not dare say so. And now the whole nation—pulpit and all—will take up the war-cry and shout itself hoarse, and mob any honest man who ventures to open his mouth; and presently such mouths will cease to open."[15] For every time you find an inquisition you find editors and politicians and preachers justifying it by saying, "We are imperiled."

When we can make a half-hero out of a subaqueous growth like Whittaker Chambers,[16] and a half-heroine out of a broomstick crackpot like Hester McCullough, and then place a government employee under charges because unidentified informants alleged that "his convictions on the question of civil rights extended slightly beyond that of the average individual," it is time to call a halt.

"Risk for risk," the wonderfully named Judge Learned Hand writes, "for myself I had rather take my chance that some traitors will escape detection than spread abroad a spirit of general suspicion and distrust...."[17] "I do not believe in democracy," Mr. Herbert U. Nelson of the National Association of Real Estate Boards differed during a congressional hearing. "I think it stinks."

Between the pretense and the piety. Between the H Bomb and the A.

Risk for risk, for myself I had rather take my chance that some traitors will escape detection than spread abroad a spirit of general suspicion and distrust, which accepts rumor and gossip in place of undismayed and unintimidated inquiry. I believe that that community is already in process of dissolution where each man begins to eye his neighbor as a possible enemy, where nonconformity with the accepted creed, political as well as religious, is a mark of disaffection; where denunciation, without specification or backing, takes the place of evidence; where orthodoxy chokes freedom of dissent; where faith in the eventual supremacy of reason has become so timid that we dare not enter our convictions in the open lists, to win or lose. Such fears as these are a solvent that can eat out the cement that binds the stones together; they may in the end subject us to a despotism as evil as any that we dread; and they can be allayed only in so far as we refuse to proceed on suspicion, and trust one another until we have tangible ground for misgiving. The mutual confidence on which all else depends can be maintained only by an open mind and a brave reliance upon free discussion. I do not say that these will suffice; who knows but we may be on a slope which leads down to

*aboriginal savagery. But of this I am sure: if we are to escape, we
must not yield a foot upon demanding a fair field and an honest
race to all ideas.*

—Judge Learned Hand,
Speech given at the University of the State of New York, Albany
October 24, 1952[18]

III.

L EAVING AMERICAN WRITERS TODAY WITH a choice easier for some than for others. "I try to give pleasure to the reading public," suggests Mr. Frank Yerby, smiling pleasantly: "The novelist has no right to impose his views on race and religion and politics upon his reader. If he wants to preach he should get a pulpit. I mean all this," the Emmett Kelly of American letters adds, "from a professional, artistic point of view."[19]

"To think that it is the duty of literature to pluck the pearl from the heap of villains is to deny literature itself," Chekhov has to put in his nickel's worth. "Literature is called artistic when it depicts life as it actually is....a writer is not a confectioner, not a cosmetician, not an entertainer."[20] Take your change and leave, Anton, there's somebody knocking at the door.

"Now when I read *Anna Karenina,*" Mr. Yerby shows Chekhov out to have a fatherly chat with Tolstoy, "I find myself skipping the peasant-in-relation-to-the-land parts. That sort of thing just isn't the novelist's job."

How come the Duke in relation to the Duchess,

that sort of thing, is the novelist's job? How come Kelly never skips those parts? If the peasant in relation to the land isn't the novelist's affair, it must follow that the city man's relationship to the street he lives on isn't any skin off his hide either. What, indeed, comes of any inquiry into the street upon which humanity—including Kelly—lives? If it isn't the writer's task to relate mankind to the things of the earth, it must be his job to keep them unrelated—lest he find himself passing not safe and dry-shod, but in angry waters up to his ears and no shoreline in sight.

What Kelly is struggling to say, from "a professional, artistic point of view," is that the chief thing is not to be seen in shabby company. Like Kafka's advocate, he feels that "the only sensible thing was to adapt oneself to existing conditions.... One's own interests would be immeasurably injured by attracting the attention of the ever-vengeful officials. Anything rather than that!"[21] To be, indeed, precisely the man Fitzgerald feigned so mordantly to admire, one of those who say "business is business" and "I'm not the person to see about that." For Fitzgerald himself became so submerged in the waters that have no shore that he had at last in anguish and bewilderment to ask why he had "become identified with the objects of my horror or compassion."[22]

Thinking of Melville, of Whitman and Jack London and Stephen Crane, Bierce and Sandburg and Mark Twain, it would seem there is no way of becoming a serious writer in the States without keeping shabby company. Thinking of Poe and Fitzgerald, Hart Crane and Vachel Lindsay, Lafcadio Hearn and George Sterling,[23] it would seem there is no way of becoming such a writer without becoming a victim.

The flabbiness and complacency of American writing at the very moment when the Italians and the French have so much sinew and fire can be accounted for, in part, by this same scorn of shabby company. Our practice of specializing our lives to let each man be his own department, safe from the beetles and the rain, is what is really meant by "a professional, artistic point of view." For it is not a point of view at all, but only a camouflaged hope that each man may be an island sufficient to himself. Thus may one avoid being brushed, even perhaps bruised, by the people who live on that shabby back street where nearly all humanity now lives.

A view that betrays an uneasy dread of other men's lives; a terror, bone-deep yet unadmitted, of the living moment. Nothing could be more alien to our Stateside lives than Gide's belief that every instant is precious because, in each, eternity is mirrored.[24] To our businessman's morality such a view is so repugnant it must be declared out of bounds; for it mocks the faith of all true believers that no virtues are greater than thrift, self-preservation and piety.

"If your God is forgetful of your life," the novelist Jean-Baptiste Rossi puts it better than Gide, "keep your life. Your life is all that matters." All that matters among the things of man's own earth. Where the life that does no more than maintain itself, denies itself.

The American middle class's faith in personal comfort as an end in itself is, in essence, a denial of life. And it has been imposed upon American writers and playwrights strongly enough to cut them off from their deeper sources.

The shortcut to comfort is called "specialization," and in an eye-ear-nose-and-throat doctor this makes sense. But in a writer it is fatal. The less he sees of other writers the more of a writer he will ultimately become. When he sees scarcely anyone except other writers, he is ready for New York. If he is already there, he will go to work for Fleur Cowles.[25] We feel it to be only one more fact of our matter-of-fact morality that birds of a feather *ought* to flock together. Thus, out of a conviction that every man should be his own department we have specialized ourselves into a condition where every man is actually his own broom closet.

That "that sort of thing" is not the novelist's job is true only in so far as it is the novelist's primary consideration to be clean-shaven and well-pressed with the brass of all his little buttons sparkling. Mr. Yerby reduced the art of writing to a ballroom game of seeing who can serve the heaviest tipper the fastest. Like any hotel manager, he demands that writers disregard what is true in the world, and real, in order to dedicate their lives to the guests. What a bellhop here was lost to the world.

No book was ever worth the writing that wasn't

done with the attitude that "this ain't what you rung for, Jack—but it's what you're damned well getting." "A novelist who would think himself of a superior essence to other men would miss the first condition of his calling," Conrad tells us.[26] Not to say that an American writer cannot keep his faith that staying warm and dry-shod is the main thing, and still write honestly. Who can say that the works of Clarence Budington Kelland[27] are anything but honest?

A line of reasoning that ought to bring an Academy Award this year to Zsa-Zsa Gabor and a Nobel Prize for Literature to Louis Bromfield. How do you know you don't have talent till you try? Openings in a big new field for young people with pleasing personalities. Send for our Aptitude Test. Take our short easy course. Learn while you earn. You too can be an artist and go to parties with the swells.

"By a long, immense and reasoned derangement of the senses," Rimbaud decided, "the poet makes himself a seer. By seeking in himself all forms of love, pain and madness, by turning himself into the great sick man, the great criminal, the great accursed, the poet reaches the unknown; and if, maddened, he should end by losing understanding of his visions, at least he has seen them."[28]

"What I get out of it financially doesn't come under consideration at all," Kelly assures us. "I write what I feel and think." Obsession remains the price of creation and the writer who declines that risk will come up with nothing more creative than *The Foxes of Harrow* or *Mrs. Parkington.*[29]

So obsessed, he will perceive that the true shore lies against the tides of his own time. If he is not to betray himself he will have to move against that current. Even though aware that the hour he'll find land will be that one when the waters toss his blue and bloated carcass up. Perhaps upon those very sands where those who play the safer game are drinking Cuba libres under beach umbrellas, murmuring contentedly, "I'm sorry, but I'm not the person to see about that" and "business *is* business."

...A novelist who would think himself of a superior essence to other men would miss the first condition of his calling. To have the gift of words is no such great matter. A man furnished with a long-range weapon does not become a hunter or a warrior by the mere possession of a firearm; many other qualities of character and temperament are necessary to make him either one or the other. Of him from whose armory of phrases one in a hundred thousand may perhaps hit the far-distant and elusive mark of art, I would ask that in his dealings with mankind he should be capable of giving a tender recognition to their obscure virtues. I would not have him impatient with their small failings and scornful of their errors. I would not have him expect too much gratitude from that humanity whose fate, as illustrated in individuals, it is open to him to depict as ridiculous or terrible. I would wish him to look with a large forgiveness at men's ideas and prejudices, which are by no means the outcome of malevolence, but depend on their education, their social status, even their professions.... I would wish him to enlarge his sympathies by patient and loving observation while he grows in mental power. It is in the impartial practice of life, if anywhere, that the promise of perfection for his art can be found

rather than in the absurd formulas trying to prescribe this or that
particular method of technique or conception. Let him mature the
strength of his imagination among the things of this earth....

—Joseph Conrad,

from an essay entitled "Books"

1905[30]

IV.

SUMMER ON SEVENTY-FIRST STREET, when I was a Southside sprout, was blue as peace. The cross above St. Columbanus caught the light of a holier daybreak than ours while the wan gas-flares still wavered. Then the bells of early mass rang out, for our own morning had lightened the alleys at last.

And long after the twilight's last lamplighter had passed, ladder across his handlebars and gas-torch against his shoulder, somebody else's twilight burned on behind that cross. The light that lingered, the light that held, belonged to somebody else's night. Somebody else's somebody else, who ran daybreak and evening too.

But not the hours that ran between. The wan little flares that the lamplighter left, the flares that tried all night to shine—then faltered and flicked out one by one—belonged to us like the alleys.

Wherever they led, the alleys were ours, and all their littered spoils. Between that early alien light and that twilight like a spell, we patrolled those battleways bearing gas-grenades made of garbage wrapped tightly in the tricolors of the *Saturday Evening Blade*.[31] We had had enough of peace.

Beside the armored schoolyard, behind the guarded bars, we tracked the treacherous Hun. Keeping one eye peeled for the barbarous Turk as well. Our bayonets were hewed from sunflower stalks: we had had enough of peace. Now we were out for blood. And on the heights of the Rock Island tracks we lost Chateau-Thierry to six anemic Swedes. (The solitary triumph of modern Swedish arms.) When we refilled the grenades from the deepest cans and crept out to the counterattack, one of us fastened a rusty wire onto an empty tomato can, pulled it through the schoolyard fence and hooked it onto a grapefruit tin: the field telephone had been invented at last.

What's more, it worked. By lying prostrate you could communicate with the courier on the other side of the fence and still stay out of the line of fire. You could, of course, have stood up and told him over the wood what you had in mind. You might, for example, have suggested, "Peace, it's wonderful"—but we were sick to death of peace. And lying prostrate was infinitely more strategic.

The accurate ear and the retentive memory of such a writer as James T. Farrell constitute a kind of literary field-telephone, a two-party line possessing the added advantage of getting a message down straight without getting smacked in the teeth with a hatful of slops. A method based on the judicious non-com's understanding that if you can keep from getting hit long enough, you'll still be passing water when the war is done. As well as upon the sensible novelist's premise that if you can nail your literary fences high enough and get enough code down behind them fast enough, the end result *must* be art.

It must be art because it pays so well.

Where the morning-report school succeeds is in its stenographic fidelity. Where it fails is in affording the breath of life to its morning reports.

Thus while Scott Fitzgerald's people possess considerably more standup vitality than those you met last night at your analyst's house-party, Farrell's, like inkblots arranged by Rorschach, own even less. Flat as the print, prostrate as one of his own shattered infinitives, Studs Lonigan no longer requires serious criticism. The most he can bear by now is an autopsy.

What Fitzgerald risked, that the field-telephone school dares not, was an emotional sharing of the lives he recorded. "I have asked a lot of my emotions," he once took mournful count, "—one hundred and twenty stories. The price was high, right up there with Kipling, because there was one little drop of something—not blood, not a tear, not my seed, but me more intimately than these, in every story, it was the extra I had. Now it has gone and I am just like you now."[32]

But he wasn't like you or me, or James T. Farrell, or anybody. He stood on the precipitous edge of exhaustion, a man who had spent himself, by coins of pity and love and pride, into spiritual bankruptcy—"I only wanted absolute quiet to think out... why I had become identified with the objects of my horror or compassion."[33]

Infected as younger writers are today by the current passion for caution in everything, the reportorial method affords an emotional detachment that makes a virtue of stenography. The advantage of replacing the complexity and the pain of the living experience with the painless and simple process of giving dictation has become sufficiently plain to the sensible writer. For by this method one could report on the overburdened without identifying himself with them. One could preserve a sense of superiority to the dead and the overburdened. A surefire means, it seemed, wherewith to gain one's art without losing one's life.

Yet time's terrible eraser sweeps the board swiftly of the names of those who succeeded, like Tarkington,[34] by never taking the risk of failure. But out of the shambles that he made of his personal life, Fitzgerald's art triumphed. Unsaving of spirit and heart and brain, he served the lives of which he wrote rather than allowing himself to be served by them.

And so died like a scapegoat, died like a victim, his work unfinished, his hopes in ruin. "...The natural state of the sentient adult," he wrote, "is a qualified unhappiness."[35]

The price had been higher than Kipling's.

O*ne harassed and despairing night I packed a briefcase and went off a thousand miles to think it over. I took a dollar room in a drab little town where I knew no one and sunk all the money I had with me in a stock of potted meat, crackers and apples. But don't let me suggest that the change from a rather overstuffed world to a comparative asceticism was any Research Magnificent—I only wanted absolute quiet to think out why I had developed a sad attitude toward sadness, a melancholy attitude toward melancholy and a tragic attitude toward tragedy*—why I had become identified with the objects of my horror or compassion.

Does this seem a fine distinction? It isn't: identification such as this spells the death of accomplishment. It is something like this that keeps insane people from working. Lenin did not willingly endure the sufferings of his proletariat, nor Washington of his troops, nor Dickens of his London poor. And when Tolstoy tried some such merging of himself with the objects of his attention, it was a fake and a failure. I mention these because they are the men best known to us all....

My self-immolation was something sodden-dark. It was very distinctly not modern—yet I saw it in others, saw it in a dozen men of honor and industry since the war.... I had stood by while one famous contemporary of mine played with the idea of the Big Out for half a year; I had watched when another, equally eminent, spent months in an asylum unable to endure any contact with his fellow-men. And of those who had given up and passed on I could list a score.

This led me to the idea that the ones who had survived had made some sort of clean break. This is a big word and is no parallel to a jailbreak when one is probably headed for a new jail or will be forced back to the old one.... A clean break is something you cannot come back from; that is irretrievable because it makes the past cease to exist. So, since I could no longer fulfill the obligations that life had set for me or that I had set for myself, why not slay the empty shell who had been posturing at it for four years? I must continue to be a writer because that was my only way of life, but I would cease any attempts to be a person—to be kind, just or generous....

I have now at last become a writer only. The man I had persistently tried to be became such a burden that I have "cut him loose".... Let the soldiers be killed and enter immediately into the Valhalla of their profession. That is their contract with the gods. A

writer need have no such ideals unless he makes them for himself,
and this one has quit.

—F. Scott Fitzgerald,
"Handle with Care," autobiographical fragment in *The Crack-Up*
April, 1936[36]

V.

NOT THAT FITZGERALD OR ANY-
one else ever forged a novel out of nothing but pity and personal recklessness.
You don't write a novel out of sheer pity
any more than you blow a safe out of a
vague longing to be rich. Compassion is all to the good, but
vindictiveness is the verity Faulkner forgot: the organic
force in every creative effort, from the poetry of Villon to
the Brinks Express Robbery, that gives shape and color to
all our dreams.

"Vice, as vice, is bad and unwanted," the French
light-heavyweight philosopher, Carpentier, once philoso-
phized, "but there must be deep down in the makeup of
every fighter a kind of viciousness. Wells (Bombardier
Wells) had me *in extremis* but he failed to see red." Marking
the only known instance of a fighter speaking Latin to the
working press, as well as the only known instance of an
English heavyweight having anyone on earth *in extremis*.

Leo Durocher, a utility infielder with a resonant
baritone, put it somewhat less literally: "I don't get this stuff

about sportsmanship. You play to win, don't you? Say I'm playing short and Mother is on first and the batter singles to right. Mother comes fast around second with the winning run—Mother will have to go down. I'll help her up, dust her off and say 'Mom, I'm sorry, but it was an accident'—but she won't of scored. Nobody asks how you happened to lose. All they want to know is did you win. If I'm spitting at a crack in the wall for nickels I still want to win. Anybody can come in second. Nice guys finish last."[37]

A certain ruthlessness and a sense of alienation from society is as essential to creative writing as it is to armed robbery. The strong-armer isn't out merely to turn a fast buck any more than the poet is out solely to see his name on the cover of a book, whatever satisfaction that event may afford him. What both need most deeply is to get even.

And, of course, neither will. Whether or not either has actually been robbed by society is beside the point. A man so convinced, however illogically, will endure the agonies of the damned to get his own back. For if he felt he had nothing coming he'd be out of business, as strong-armer or poet, that same day.

If you feel you belong to things as they are, you won't hold up anybody in the alley no matter how hungry you may get. And you won't write anything that anyone will read a second time either. "The artist must approach his work in the same frame of mind in which the criminal commits his deed," Degas agreed in essence with Durocher.

In the more meaningful writing, as in the defter sort of jack-rolling, this is either candid or concealed. Candid as in Céline, Genet or Dorothy Parker, concealed as in Koestler, Richard Wright or Mickey Spillane. And in the very best writing the one becomes a complete sublimation of the other.

"Even then," Dostoevsky's underground man recalls, "I carried this hole in the floor of my heart. I was terribly afraid to be seen and recognized."[38]

The great paradox of Dostoevsky lies in the vitality he drew from degradation. American writing, it is this observer's notion, will remain without vigor until it draws upon the enormous reservoir of sick, vindictive life that moves like an underground river beneath all our boulevards. When the sewers back up we call it a "crime wave;" when after a while the waters subside a little we are content until the waters begin to lap the curb again. Then the pumps come out, and we're in for another wave of reforms, from press, pulpit and politician, which serve to increase newspaper circulation, fill up the pews for a few Sundays and pump up the local payrolls.

The stranger from Mars who spent a day in the public library came away knowing that a few Americans possessed wealth that was virtually incalculable, that a hundred-odd million others had more than just enough. But gained barely an inkling into the lives of those who live out their hand-to-mouth hours without friendship or love.

They belong to no particular street in no particular city. They pass from furnished room to furnished room, and belong not even to their own time; not even to themselves. They are the ones who are displaced in time, and again displaced in the heart....

"I read the smooth journals but they gave no news of this."

Not until he walked the unswept streets in the hundred-storied evening and saw the legend in the first-floor-front—ROOM FOR TRANSIENT—did he begin to understand. Or was advised by a clerk, across an ancestral register, "Give a phony, mister." He wanted to say who he was, but the clerk didn't want to know.

Not until he saw them sleeping in the all-night restaurants and the all-night movies and the night-blue bars of the whiskey wilderness did he understand at last that he was on the ancient unswept street where most of humanity has always lived.

And had he asked them, they would not have been able to say who they were. Belonging nowhere, no one can tell who he really is. Who one really is depends on what world he belongs to. The secret multitudes who belong to no world, no way of life, no particular time and place, are the truly displaced persons: displaced from their true selves. They are not the disinherited: they are those who have disinherited their own selves.

Out of the furnished rooms and into a cheap hotel

and back to the furnished room before the room is out: the "unemployed bartender," "unemployed short-order cook," "unemployed salesman," "unemployed model," "unemployed hostess;" "self-styled actor," "self-styled artist," "self-styled musician," "self-styled author," as the self-styled reporters conveniently file them. Their names are the names of certain dreams from which the light has gone out.

The clerk at the third-rate hotel is always half-pleased to see the "unemployed hostess" or "self-styled actress" come in to register, wearing nylon hose and carrying all she owns in the handbag slung over her shoulder. "A room with a private bath," she instructs him. "I don't want to be disturbed." You don't have to tell *her* to give a phony.

He isn't even half-pleased to see her, two decades further along, in black ribbed-wool stockings and a shopping bag. But her manner is more humble. "I'll pay in advance," she offers, before anybody throws her out. "You certainly will," he assures her.

Give her another decade and she'll show up, just before daybreak, with neither handbag nor shopping; and no stockings at all. Just a weary old weirdie who would lie down to rest. "You got a checkout room for me, mister?"

Meaning any room vacated by a full-paying guest before his allotted time was up; leaving an hour, or even two or three, before somebody else able to pay rent around the clock shows up. Weary Old Weirdie gets it for half price—and into the clerk's pocket that goes, you can be mighty sure. Weirdie takes her own chances—she may be rooted out of last night's sheets in an hour. But if there's no particular run on rooms she may be left alone up there till evening.

Those are the chances you take if you're an old weirdie with most of your hours, save but a few, left behind in the disheveled sheets of a thousand checkout rooms. If nobody tells you anymore to give a phony. Knowing that even your true name has become a phony.

Wanderer untroubled by names and numbers: unregistered, unattached, uncounted and unbereaved in the files of the American Century. There are no insurance policies to bereave her, no bankbook to grieve her, no driver's license nor visa, no hospitalization plan nor social security number to say, the day after the nameless burial, what her true name was. Nothing but the hardwood subway bench and the Twelfth Street Station to remember: W. O. Weirdie once took rest here.

Self-styled actress; self-styled stunt man; self-styled world traveler, part-time entertainer and full-time veteran; self-styled heiress: their names are no more than the names of certain lonely hours. They sought someone to tell who they were, and never found anyone; for they did not know themselves who they were. They looked whole lifetimes for an answer without knowing what the question was.

The pool shark hitchhiking to Miami or Seattle, the fruit pickers following the crops in a 1939 Chevy with one headlight gone and the other cracked; carny-men and pitch-men, punchboard operators and unemployed blackjack dealers; pigeon-droppers and penny-matchers, young touts in Hollywood tattersalls and coneroos from the Good Old Days in dirty London collars; freelancing phonies and necktie salesmen with furtive eyes; and the stripper forced to a stint of secret hustling after the Super Breakfast show is done, to get up her Daddy's fine because Daddy's doing thirty days for going on the drunk again. (Daddy would blow his top, she boasts, if he knew what she was doing. It's all right so long as he's allowed to pretend he doesn't dig a thing. Daddy is smart enough not to ask questions and Baby is smart enough to act as though there were none to ask. It makes things easier for Daddy. And what's good for Daddy is good for the country.)[39]

These aren't the great gray wolves that run the winter wilderness, but only the toothless, half-tame jackals that prowl the outskirts of dude-ranch camps when night-fires start to wane. Hard-time nomads or easy-livers, zigzag zanies or phony martyrs, young band-rats or elderly satyrs who buy a little and sell a little, work a day and rest a while. Sleep by day and play by night, they abide in an evening country where ten a.m. always looks more like five in the afternoon of any season at all. Theirs is that ancestral hour when the little deeds are done.

All those who, between sleep and selling, between rest by day and play by night, do the little deals.

"But do you know," somewhere one of Dostoevsky's odd fish cries out suddenly, "do you know it is impossible to charge man with sins, to burden him with debts and turning the other cheek, when society is organized so meanly that man cannot help but perpetrate villainies; when, economically, he has been brought to villainy, and that it is silly and cruel to demand from man that which, by the very laws of nature, he is impotent to perform even if he wished to...?"[40]

Their names are those of certain nighttime notions, held too tightly, that would not ever have been conceived had there been someone in the night to hold instead.

And do their time cheerfully enough when trapped—thirty days or sixty or ninety without a hangover of guilt. The little man in the business suit who wouldn't steal a dime if you put it in his pocket carries around a heavier load of guilt these days than do the people of the twilight. When the latter take a fall they come out ready to say, "I paid for that one," for they feel they have. But the business suit, when he is finished paying in full for everything, is plagued by the feeling that there's something unpaid for yet. So he goes to a twenty-dollar-an-hour analyst who feels guiltier than he does. Americans everywhere face gunfire better than guilt.

It is the hapless, useless, helpless goof-ups who'd rather play a juke all day than get into the rat race for fame and fortune, who go guiltless. The tricked, the maimed and the tortured who do the little deeds. And never lie down to rest. For they sense that the guilt is elsewhere.

The caves of their country are the acres and acres of furnished rooms as well as the railroad hotels of the small-town slums; on the dim-lit streets behind the bright-lit boulevards as on the rutted roads behind Main Street; in the chicken-wire flops as in the all-steel cells with the solid doors; backroom brothels as in back-street bars; in the courts and the wards and the charity hospitals; in all the dens and all the dives wherein we see and touch the bone and flesh out of which our time is forged at last.

Down in the alley battleways behind the billboards with the painted smiles.

There, accustomed to taking daily strolls along the unterraced edge of utter disaster, long used to being booted gratuitously by the hindquarters of destruction, here at last are all those, in Dostoevsky's phrase, for whom nobody prays: the ones whose defeats cost everything of real value, and yet whose laughter cuts closest to the bone.

Leaving scar-tissue enough to satisfy Ilsa Koch.

In the horse-and-wagon alleyways of the littered hinterland behind the editorials. The street that stenography so often reports yet never can touch without flinching. The unswept streets where most of humanity has always lived.

Yet, in suggesting that the true climate of the human condition on the home grounds may best be gauged underground, I'm referring not only to a sociological strata but to a psychological condition as well: all those so submerged emotionally that they are unable to belong to the world in which they live.

"To regard the universe as one's own," Simone de Beauvoir writes, "one must belong to the caste of the privileged; it is for those alone who are in command to justify the universe by changing it, by thinking about it, by revealing it..."[41] To know oneself one must belong to the world.

It is therefore possible to live underground even while skiing at Aspen or Sun Valley. You don't have to live in an alley to be submerged.

Although, come to think of it, that does seem as good a way as any of going about it.

was in penal servitude, and I saw "desperate" criminals. I repeat, this was a hard school. Not one of them ceased to consider himself a criminal. To look at, they were a dreadful and cruel lot. However, only the simpletons and newcomers were "braggarts," and these used to be ridiculed. Mostly, they were gloomy, pensive people. No one spoke about his crimes. I never heard any grumbling. It was even impossible to speak aloud about one's crimes. Now and then someone would utter a word with a challenge and a twist—and all the inmates, as one man, would "put a check on" the pert fellow. It was a rule not to speak about this. Nevertheless, I believe, probably not one among them evaded long psychic suffering within himself—that suffering that is the most purifying and invigorating. I saw them solitarily pensive; I beheld them in the church, praying before confession; I listened to their single, spontaneous words and exclamations; I remember their faces—and, believe me, not one of them, in his innermost, considered himself right!

—Fyodor Dostoevsky,
from *The Diary of a Writer*
1873[42]

VI.

FROM THE PENTHOUSE SUSPENDED silently so high above the winding traffic's iron lamentation, forty straight-down stories into those long, low, night-blue bars aglow below street-level, a lonely guilt pervades us all.

A loneliness not known to any ancestral land. To some other less cautious race conquering or lost. No other age, more distant and less troubled. No other time, less lonely and much longer. No other night-blue bars.

No other forest of the night, no other wilderness than ours.

Ours no longer being the lonesome prairie's desolation, but the spiritual desolation of men and women made incapable of using themselves for anything more satisfying than the promotion of chewing gum, a goo with a special ingredient or some detergent ever-urgent. Working one trap or another for others, the aging salesman of bonds or used cars having made his little pile, senses dimly that he's backed up into a trap of his own devising.

The tiger-pit of loneliness out of which there is no

climbing. Alone at last with his little pile, the weary years in and the weary years out haven't brought him a thing he wanted in his heart. It was only that which he was taught he was supposed to desire that he now owns so uselessly.

"It is because of the abstract climate in which they live that the importance of money is so disproportionate," Simone de Beauvoir observes. "The people are neither mean nor avaricious.... If money is the sole object for so many, it is because the other values have been reduced to this one denominator."[43]

The criticism is valid but neglects those rebels, from penthouse to bar, who resist, every hour on the hour, success according to that cult. All those who feel their hours to be too brief to devote to the working of traps. In them the desire to be of real use in the world deadlocks with the carking dread of being used by it. Habit has made it impossible for them to exist beyond the boundaries of the cult. Contemptuous of a philosophy that preaches that every man is an island and each man's duty is to appoint his private island comfortably, they are, even while being most contemptuous, unable to live except on an island and simply cannot endure the discomfort of living anywhere else.

The most bitter protest against the middle-class faith in money as an end in itself always comes, in the States, from the children of that class, who have to take the spiritual consequences of having too much of everything though earning nothing, while those who work hard all their lives never have enough of anything. Trapped between the double tyrannies of conscience and personal comfort, comfort wins going away. The bitter protest is drowned at last in that self-pity that abides at the bottom of the nearest pinch bottle of Haig & Haig.

"It isn't that young Americans don't wish to do great things," Mme. de Beauvoir adds, "but that they don't know there are great things to be done."[44] Not what they desire most deeply, but what, for lack of a better goal, they are forced to settle for.

From the coolest zoot-suit cat getting leaping-drunk on straight gin to the gentlest suburban matron getting discreetly tipsy on Alexanders, the feeling is that of having too much of something not really needed, and nothing at all of something needed desperately. They both want to live, and neither knows how. That's the trap.

A trap in which some turn to that same twenty-dollar-an-hour analyst—"Doctor, what's my problem?" And the doctor cannot speak the truth without losing his double saw. To stiff-arm a customer with the alarm that his trouble is something as simple as cowardice, or as hopeless as a spiritual void, would be only to lose that twenty an hour to a competitor with a more flattering tale to tell. After all, a doctor has problems too. Particularly when he's in the same secret trap as the patient—his sole advantage being, as in dealing blackjack, that he's on the side of the house.

The more daring man decides to throw over his

job and get howling drunk: success is for squares, have a ball while you can, tomorrow be damned and all of that.

Yet Monday morning finds him back at his desk pushing that real good goo, the crazy kind with the special flavor, the hair oil that leads to early promotion, the cologne that makes the girls want to take you to stag parties or the booze that affords every Clark Street lush with his fly unbuttoned a certain distinguished air.

"When something does not go well with us, we seek for causes outside of ourselves," Chekhov observed. "Capital, masons, the Syndicate, the Jesuits, bugaboos, are ghosts....If the French start talking about the Yids, the Syndicate, it is a sign that they feel all is not well with them, that a worm is gnawing at them, that they need these ghosts to appease their disturbed consciences."[45]

Something is gnawing, so somebody has to be punished. For those who need to rebel, but cannot afford it, the scapegoats who live at the bottom of a whiskey bottle will do. For those to whom drink or drugs or dice are unthinkable, Joe McCarthy is the boy with the proper answers.

Some rebels.

The addict's revolt has a special grace. When he shoves a needle into his vein it is, in a sense, to spare others. Somebody had to be punished all right—and he's the first who's got it coming. Things are going wrong in the world, so, in a sort of suicidal truculence, he impales himself.

That the truculence of the witch-hunter is something else is evidenced by the ferreting into all our hearts.

When Faulkner fitted out his workshop, being a good American didn't mean just being a good non-com. Now the notion seems to be that what matters most is how to pilot a jet or strip a bazooka, and that that is all that really matters.

"I went into the army," I heard the teenage volunteer explaining himself, "because that's where they can't fire me."

"All I want," another decides, "is a job with a pension to it." But why the undertone of disappointment, the dull unacknowledged pang, as though everything he had ever done was only what he had been told to do and out of it all he had yet had nothing all for himself? As if, each time he took an order, he felt that same dull pang.

"I know right from wrong," a girl in trouble tells me, "but I don't seem able to get a foot on the ground either way."

They'd rather take their chance in the full light of the taverns or the half-light of the lounges, these days, than among men. The teenager feels, as often as not, that there is no longer much point in knocking himself out to be a good surgeon, architect or engineer when there seems so little chance that he'll ever be able to put real skill to work. Our idealists aren't calling for those crafts as they did in Faulkner's America—they're calling for good officers and reliable non-coms, in civvies as well as in uniform.

Indeed, by packaging Success with Virtue, we make of failure a moral defeat. And rather than risk such failure, the less daring now take it to be the part of wisdom to sit it out in the booths and the bars. They do not wish to commit themselves, they are reluctant, in this sick air, to let themselves be engaged. Not realizing that the only true defeat is to be capable of playing a part in the world, and playing no part at all.

They aren't drinking, as did Faulkner's folk, out of a deep sense of personal loss, because they never had anything of their own to lose. They aren't getting drunk, like Hemingway's losers, out of disillusionment, because they never had any. They grew up in the ruins and they know the caves of their own country better than you or me or Fulton Sheen.[46] Or Fulton Lewis or Fulton Oursler or any of the other purveyors of prefabricated miracles.

The caves of a country where there are no longer universal truths, though you seek them in all the caves. All those who would have us live morally out of fear, rather than from a sense of inner freedom.

From the penthouse suspended silently forty straight-down stories into the long, low night-blue bars, they've put the line about God and Country on the same shelf as the one about "What is good for General Motors is good for the country." Or "be loyal to the company, son, and you'll be managing a branch office before you're forty."

They aren't having heart-to-heart talks with the minister anymore. Look at the minister and you'll see why.

If you want to go for that dead-end about the branch office yourself, goodbye, good luck and God bless you—but don't try dragging this cat along.

"There is no more universal idea," Dostoevsky complained, being a plaintive sort anyhow. "Everything is flabby, vapid! We all, we all are empty!"

That, of course, was in another country. And besides, God is dead.

Part-time bartender; part-time philosopher; part-time recording artist. Self-styled record mimic, self-styled song-stylist. Part-time madam, full-time madman.

In the full light of the taverns or the half-light of the lounges.

*S*itting with N. A. [Nelson Algren] in a quiet little
bar I missed half what he was saying, and I felt that
his difficulties were not less than mine. He hesitated
about what to show me in Chicago. There were no worthwhile bands
to listen to, the middle-class nightclubs were no more interesting than
those of New York, and the idea of a musical show did not appeal to
me. If I liked, he could take me to places where probably I should not
have the occasion to venture; he could give me a glimpse of the lowest
districts in Chicago, for he knew them well. I accepted.

He took me to West Madison Avenue, which is also called
the Bowery of Chicago; here are the lodging-houses for men only, flop-
houses, squalid bars. It was very cold, the street was almost deserted;
and yet there were a few men with shipwrecked faces who hid themselves in the shadows of the doorways or wandered up and down the
frozen sidewalks. We entered a bar that reminded me of Sammy's
Follies: but there was neither show nor spectators, and no tourist other
than myself. N. A. was not a tourist, for he often came here and knew
all the people, hoboes, drunks and faded beauties: no one would turn
round even if the Mad Woman of Chaillot came in. At the end of the
room there was a little negro band; one read on a placard: "It is forbid-

den to dance"; but people were dancing. There was a lame man who waddled about like a duck: suddenly he started to dance and his legs obeyed him: he spun round, jumped and capered about with a maniacal smile; it seemed he spent his time here and danced all night. Sitting at the bar was a woman with long, fine hair adorned with a red ribbon; sometimes her hair was blond, and her doll's face was that of a little girl; sometimes her head seemed covered with white tow; she was a siren well over sixty; she drank one beer after another out of the bottle while talking to herself and shouting defiantly; sometimes she got up and danced, lifting her skirts very high. A drunk asleep at a table woke up and seized a fat floozy in his arms; they capered around and danced deliriously. There was something of madness and ecstasy; so old, so ugly, so miserable, they were lost for a moment and they were happy. I felt bewildered, stared and said: "It's beautiful." N. A. was astounded; it seemed to him very French. "With us," he said, "ugliness and beauty, the grotesque and the tragic, and even good and evil, go their separate ways: Americans do not like to think that such extremes can mingle."

—Simone de Beauvoir,
from *American Day by Day*
February 21st, 1947[47]

VII.

"HOW DID YOU GET ON STUFF IN THE first place?" the judge would like to know. "There was so many little troubles floatin' around," the girl not yet twenty explains, "I figured why not roll them all up into one big trouble?"

"*Why* a young girl like you should want to live like this I simply fail to understand," his honor simply fails to understand.

"Don't bother me with why I got to live any way at all," not-yet-twenty begs off, "Just tell me *how* for God's sake."

"Don't you *care* what happens to you?"

"Why should I?" she warns the courtroom quietly, "All I have to do is shove a paper of strychnine into my next hype, then you'll all die."

Next case.

"What do you do all day?" the judge wants to know of a sixteen-year-old boy who was, until six months ago, a high-school sophomore.

"I just lean," the kid from Cloudland, still adrift, answers dreamily, "I just find a hallway or washroom 'n' take a shot. Then I lean. Just lean 'n' dream."

"Don't you care what happens to you?"

"It don't matter what happens to me. Because all the time it's really happening to someone else."

Somebody else's somebody else who doesn't matter at all.

Watching a jackal from Dallas having a breakfast consisting of five bennies, five Nembutals and two and a half grains of morphine—"How can you walk with all that stuff in you?" is what I'd like to know.

"How can I walk without it?" is what Dallas would like to know.

"I don't believe in them squares," a woman heroin peddler warns me just for my own good, "I'm scared to death of the way they live. I don't even know what they're laughin' at. 'Specially when they *laugh* at Johnny Ray.[48] He makes me cry. I don't mean real tears of course. People on Stuff are too dry-eyed to cry like squares. But I cry when they laugh at him all the same."

The twisted anguish of the singer, too lonesome for real tears—"He may not be a cat hisself, but he know how us cats got to suffer."

Blame it on the comic books, blame it on the Communists. Blame it on Costello or Lucky Luciano.[49] Blame it on the people who peddle if that makes you feel easier. Blame it on the police or the passing of the old-fashioned Sunday School.

But these are all results and not causes at all: only names we employ to exculpate ourselves. We are willing, in our right-mindedness, to lend money or compassion—but never so right-minded as to permit ourselves to be personally involved in anything so ugly. We'll pay somebody generously to haul garbage away but we cannot afford to admit that it belongs to us. We have deported the high-school sprout to Cloudland by right-mindedness.

"You think The Nab don't want the traffic to go on as it is?" another pusher challenges me, "with the loot that's in it for them? They never had it so good. If the squares didn't want people to be on stuff nobody would be on it. Who do you think The Nab is working for—them or us?

"It's the squares make the laws that make it so hard on us cats—but all them laws do is to make it that much harder on their own fool selves in the end. When they bear down they make our risk bigger, so the payoff goes higher. It costs just that much more to stay in business. So the junkie got to come up with more gold than ever, and there's only one place he can get it. Off the square. Why shouldn't we get to them?

"We do without family or friends, we give up everything. When The Nab catches us broke, the only lawyer we can get is one who's on the other side. Ain't nobody on the junkie's side. Not even other junkies.

"Them squares, they walk around free. But us cats got to suffer."

"How'd you get on stuff in the first place, pusher?"

"Too much vitality, cat. Vitality was runnin' away with me. I'd go three days without sleep 'n' knock off two hours 'n' be ready to take off again. Got into all sorts of hell for no reason but just to make something happen. Now I go two hours 'n' I'm ready to knock off for three days. It's how to stay out of trouble."

"I didn't get on because of too much pep," a contrary cat has a different tale. "I got on it because everybody I knew was making sixty-seventy a week and I couldn't make more'n thirty-five. Some days I couldn't lay by a dime. Now some days I make more than that before noon. It makes a real little go-getter out of you."

"When one is peacefully at home," Chekhov observes, "life seems ordinary. But as soon as one walks into the streets and begins to observe and to talk to women, then life becomes truly terrible."

And when one walks into a courtroom where women are being tried, it begins to seem that they are the innocent ones. That it is His Honor, the arresting officers and that little man who stands beside His Honor whispering, "She was up before you on the same charge last week, Your Honor," as well as the indifferent spectator, who are the guilty parties.

Guilty of indifference. Guilty of self-righteousness.

Guilty of complacency.

And what did he mean, the little leaning dreamer, in saying, as he teetered, that whatever happens to him really happens to somebody else? Did he mean something like that other cat meant when she said, "I remember that particular day so well, because I felt like myself for a little while. But I don't feel like myself anymore."

They get to feeling so lonesome for their lost nameless selves, down there in the night-blue bars. "You're dragging along and you know it's the end of the end—then a strange kick hits you and nothing seems like it used to be," is how one cat puts it. "Strange kicks hook you, and the bad times are forgot." Meaning perhaps that he wants to know his own name, but that there is no one to tell him.

Strange things still happen from time to time, maybe something will happen to you that never happened to any cat before. Down in the caves of the wilderness, where the loot is large, The Nab greases easy, and they call all peddlers "Jack-the-Rabbit."

Where they know when to use bennies and when to use suckies, when to square up and when to goof. A time for M and a time for H and a time for tapering off. An evening country where ten a.m. always looks a little like five in the afternoon.

Between seven and eleven it is quiet on the street, for the cats are sleeping the strange light sleep. They have an hour now of neither fever-dreams nor fear.

Till the sleeping blood begins to stir, they wake up sneezing with watering eyes and know: Jack-the-Rabbit is on his way.

The rhythms of the junkie night are the cycle of the block, for the peddler moves as the blood cries out. "And you know it ain't habit-forming, cat," Jack-the-Rabbit assures you with a nudge. "It just makes you want to try it again."

They know what M is and what H is and what weed is better than the judges. The Nab knows, but the judges who try them in Chicago are beside themselves with ignorance. "I can tell you what a man on H will do," Judge Gibson Gorman of the local narcotics court tells an audience, "but I can't predict what he'll do on marijuana—he may commit murder and he may not."

They know when to plaster a ten-spot onto the skin, under a band-aid, to keep The Nab from getting it all.

They recognize popular songs at the juke's first summer-colored note, and ask one another solemnly, "How do you think Coleman Hawkins felt when Lester Young came along?"[50]

They know what squares never do—that every man is guilty unless, by some ruse, he can prove his innocence. They know that, in Chicago courts, it isn't a matter of discovering who is innocent, but only who is the least guilty. All this they know that no square knows. All this, and much besides.

Some, the very wisest cats of all, even know how to go to the Bridewell[51] and come out with a bigger habit than they had going in.

How do you think the Mills Brothers felt when Billy Williams came along?

These are not the disinherited. For they have disinherited their selves. And don't know where to find them.

Down here where they've found one another, in lieu of themselves, to form a loose federation of the lost. Whether God, or Christ, will ever redeem them doesn't matter any longer; because Man never will. Great things still happen from time to time so maybe something'll happen to you. How do you think Vaughn Monroe felt when Frankie Laine came along?

Unbereaved or unbereft, scoffing or debauched, the geared and the ungeared, they live out their lives like ghosts of some winter twilight when winter is nearly done.

Knowing their own faces, strong or weak. Their own poor faces, gay or bleak. Knowing the phonies as well as the true sporty-ones who are just putting it on. Knowing their own hat size, cap or tam, each being loyal to a particular brand of cigarette or bar, yet knowing there is no difference worth mentioning between any. They need to be loyal to *something,* having lost all loyalty to their true selves. But that's too big a job. They've lost their selves out there somewhere where Christ lost his shoes. How can anyone be loyal to someone you never got to know, for God's sake?

Strolling the broken stones beyond the ruins of the City of God, out where the rutted roads begin, it is rumored vaguely, here and there, that certain unnamed subdividers plan the City of Man. So between the old town and the new they go, inventing new gods along the way.

"Junk is like God," not-yet-twenty explains, "it makes a place in your heart you'll never forget. You got to be punished for believing in it, but you go on believing all the same. It's like being a martyr sort of."

Some people say that junkies lie. But it seems to me that some people who aren't even on Stuff don't tell the truth all the time either.

How do you think Gene Krupa felt when Jackie Cooper came along?

H. *E. F. Donohue: I asked you to think about American literature. What did you decide?*

Algren: Well, you asked me what's the matter with American literature and I think the trouble with American literature is it doesn't know who it is. It thinks it's Henry Miller writing to Lawrence Durrell, and then again it thinks it's James Baldwin telephoning Norman Mailer, and then it thinks it's Jack Kerouac, subsisting on Coca-Colas on a cross-country ride to nowhere—

Donohue: What is it?

Algren: Actually, American literature isn't anybody phoning to anybody or anybody writing about anybody. American literature is the woman in the courtroom who, finding herself undefended on a charge, asked, "Isn't anybody on my side?" It's also the phrase I used that was once used in court of a kid who, on being sentenced to death, said, "I knew I'd never get to be twenty-one anyhow." More recently I think American literature is also the fifteen-year-old who, after he had stabbed somebody, said, "Put me in the electric chair— my mother can watch me burn." Even more recently, American literature is a seventeen-year-old kid picked up on a double murder charge, two killings in a boat, in a ship off Miami, who said he was very glad it happened, he had absolutely no regrets, his only fear was that he might not get the electric chair. He had no vindictiveness toward those two people he killed. He said they were pretty good about it. They didn't know, they had no idea, that he was going to come up with a knife. He had, in fact, a little bit of admiration for their coolness. One of them, finding himself stabbed, said, "Why?" He wanted to know. He said, "I can't tell them why." But I know he's been trying to get out of it since he's six years old. This is an honors student, you understand, this is a bright boy from a respectable home. He never remembers a time when he wasn't fully convinced that death was better than life. And now he was very contented, his only worry being that he might not get the electric chair. He's afraid of that. That's the only fear he has, that he might have to continue to live. I think that's American literature.

—Algren and H. E. F. Donohue,
from *Conversations with Nelson Algren*
1963[52]

VIII.

"**E**VEN IF DREYFUS IS GUILTY," CHEKHOV wrote to Suvorin, "Zola nevertheless is right, because the business of writers is not to accuse, not to persecute, but to side even with the guilty, once they are condemned and suffer punishment.... Even without them there are plenty of accusers, prosecutors and gendarmes, and in any event the role of Paul suits them better than that of Saul."[53]

The function of the writer in the States as well is to champion the accused. There are already so many Junior G-men competing for posse duty that they're paying their own expenses. "If you're so innocent, what were you doing where the trouble was going on?" is the new Peglerism.[54] "If you're not guilty, what are you doing in jail? You admit you don't know the law—how can you claim to be innocent?"

When Joseph K., in Kafka's *The Trial*, charged by unidentified informants with a crime unnamed, is led at last out of the city by two strangers in top hats and propped against a boulder, one top hat draws a butcher's knife and passes it, ceremonially, across K. to the second executioner—who ceremonially passes it back in an Alphonse-and-Gaston act. "K. now perceived clearly that he was supposed to seize the knife himself, as it traveled from hand to hand above him, and plunge it into his own breast."[55]

"It may be no more than a coincidence," Representative Busbey of Illinois comments on the suicide of a State Department employee, "that he worked in a government agency where Communists, Communist sympathizers and poor loyalty risks have plagued our security.... In view of the fact that Montgomery brought his own life to an end, we should not assume that he was innocent of such associations."

For so deeply now do we presume the accused to be guilty by the act of having been accused, that it seems to us no more than an act of atonement to turn the knife on himself. The accused who stubbornly declines this form of confession is now advised that either the answers he *would* have given would have incriminated him or else he would not have declined. Refusal to reply thus becomes an automatic confession of guilt. You're damned if you do and you're damned if you don't. Leaving us with the implication that the men who devised the Fifth Amendment had in mind not the protection of the innocent, but of the guilty. How sick can you get?

That this is the same sickness as that of Salem, as has been indicated: one wherein we attempt to exorcise our devils by destroying the dissenters or odd fish of the tribe.

Our fear that Fort Worth and Oconomowoc are in imminent peril until Iceland and Morocco are armored like Fort Knox is not our true fear. If it were, the acquisition of great bases encircling the globe would greatly lessen it. But after five years of stretching our arms from the South Seas to the North Atlantic, we feel not a whit more secure than before. All we've done is to lose the trust of other peoples. We have gained a world, and lost it. When we were small, and beset by greater powers, we were less afraid. For the fear is not from monsters who walk abroad, but from monsters who walk in our own hearts.

Like Faust, we have two souls within a single breast. We profess to believe that a people may guarantee its happiness by military might, and in the same breath disclaim authoritarianism. We say the great word Democracy, and in the same breath align ourselves with Spanish, Greek, Chinese and Korean Fascism. We wish to inherit the earth, and yet have not learned to govern ourselves. We boast of our strength, yet display our fear. At the same moment that we set the world an example of corruption in our big cities unparalleled anywhere in the world, we cannot tolerate peoples governing themselves by other forms than our own. And support intolerance by plane and tank, by warship and bazooka. To paraphrase the old biblical saw, "The good that we would do we do not; but the evil which we would not, that we do."[56] And a fear of some disaster is companioned secretly within us by a yearning for that same disaster, swift and soundless. A padding dread within will not be still.

We seem to be going on the strange assumption that if we can but put our fears on a mass scale, they will, belonging thus to all of us, be somehow wiser. We have come to the point where, in order to avoid the face of our own psychosis, we insist that all good men be psychotic.

For if we have not, as a nation, gone psychotic, how is it that we now honor most those whom we once most despised? Now the professional perjurer is called an "informant"—we used to call them something else. Blackmail in the name of "anti-Communism" is now dignified by the name of "research services." Though we always believed, by and large, in rugged individualism, we didn't until now like the idea of dog eat dog. If we don't, what is the odious hulk of Fat Pat McCarran doing in the Senate? What is a man like McCarthy, whose mentality never equipped him for anything more than dealing three-card monte, doing there? Never before in our history has a man so puny-minded as Jenner been dignified by the title of Senator.

The late American humorist Jake Falstaff once did a prophetic little skit called *Alice in Justice-Land*:

> "'I hope you will not be impatient with me,'
> said Alice, 'I'm really quite interested in this sys-
> tem, and I would like to know more about it.'
>
> "'It's very sane and very human,' said the
> White Knight. 'If you hate your neighbor as you
> love yourself, you don't charge him with being a
> hateful person. You call up the police and tell them

that his automobile is parked without a taillight. That's our system exactly. Only we carry it a step farther. Our system has been made so perfect that the taillight doesn't have to be out. It can be proved that it *might* go out—that it's *potentially* out.'

"'The whole system seems to be predicated on the word might,' said Alice.

"'Might,' said the White Knight, solemnly, 'makes right.'

"'If you charge a man with the crime he really committed, your prosecution is limited to one count. But if you charge him with something else, you have the whole book of statutes to choose from.'

"'Doesn't it happen sometimes that a man gets free of everything?' Alice asked.

"'Oh, certainly. But the system provides even for that. By that time he has spent all his money on litigation, his reputation is ruined, and he has spent as much time in jail as he would have spent on the original charge anyhow.'

"'Then,' said Alice, in sad bewilderment, 'am I to understand that most of the people in jail are innocent?'

"'Every one,' said the White Knight tolerantly but wearily, 'every one in the world, my dear child, is innocent of something.'"[57]

We have come to a time, George Bernanos wrote,

when evil is in its first beginnings. A time of the disaster swift and soundless. A time for the great gray wolves that run the winter wilderness. A time when suspicion has become an honorable trade.

"There can be no doubt," Kafka's doomed wanderer decided, "that behind all the actions of this court of justice, that is to say in my case, behind my arrest and today's interrogation, there is a great organization at work... And the significance of this great organization, gentlemen? It consists in this, that innocent persons are accused of guilt, and senseless proceedings are put in motion against them...."[58]

*hen one of them opened his frock coat and out of a
sheath that hung from a belt girt round his waistcoat
drew a long, thin, double-edged butcher's knife, held
it up, and tested the cutting edges in the moonlight. Once more the
odious courtesies began, the first handed the knife across K. to the second, who handed it across K. back again to the first. K. now perceived clearly that he was supposed to seize the knife himself, as it
traveled from hand to hand above him, and plunge it into his own
breast. But he did not do so, he merely turned his head, which was
still free to move, and gazed around him. He could not completely
rise to the occasion, he could not relieve the officials of all their tasks;
the responsibility for this last failure of his lay with him who had not
left him the remnant of strength necessary for the deed. His glance fell
on the top story of the house adjoining the quarry. With a flicker as of
a light going up, the casements of a window there suddenly flew open;
a human figure, faint and insubstantial at that distance and that
height, leaned abruptly far forward and stretched both arms still farther. Who was it? A friend? A good man? Someone who sympathized?
Someone who wanted to help? Was it one person only? Or was it
mankind? Was help at hand? Were there arguments in his favor that

had been overlooked? Of course there must be. Logic is doubtless unshakable, but it cannot withstand a man who wants to go on living. Where was the Judge whom he had never seen? Where was the high Court, to which he had never penetrated? He raised his hands and spread out all his fingers.

But the hands of one of the partners were already at K.'s throat, while the other thrust the knife deep into his heart and turned it there twice. With failing eyes K. could still see the two of them immediately before him, cheek leaning against cheek, watching the final act. "Like a dog!" he said; it was as if the shame of it must outlive him.

—Franz Kafka,
from *The Trial*
1914-15[59]

IX.

"NOW GIT OUT OF THE WAY," MR. Dooley once warned us, "for here comes property, drunk 'n' raisin' Cain." When wise old kings of Egypt decided to have a ball, so I'm told, they placed a mummy at the head of the table to remind themselves, even at the height of the festivities, of their own mortality. We today might, with equal wisdom, in this our own season of celebration, nod respectfully toward John Foster Dulles.[60] Lest we too prove too proud.

For ball or no ball, any season at all, we live today in a laboratory of human suffering as vast and terrible as that in which Dickens and Dostoevsky wrote. The only real difference being that the England of Dickens and the Russia of Dostoevsky could not afford the soundscreens and the smokescreens with which we so ingeniously conceal our true condition from ourselves.

So accustomed have we become to the testimony of the photo-weeklies, backed by witnesses from radio and TV, establishing us permanently as the happiest, healthiest, sanest, wealthiest, most inventive, tolerant and fun-loving folk yet to grace the earth of man, that we tend to forget that these are bought-and-paid-for witnesses and all their testimony perjured.

For it is not in the afternoon in Naples nor yet at evening in Marseille, not in Indian hovels half-sunk in an ancestral civilization's ruined halls nor within those lion-colored tents pitched down the Sahara's endless edge that we discover those faces most debauched by sheer uselessness. Not in the backwash of poverty and war, but in the backwash of prosperity and progress.

On the back streets and the boulevards of Palm Beach and Miami, on Fifth Avenue in New York and Canal Street in New Orleans, on North Clark Street in Chicago, on West Madison or South State or any street at all in Los Angeles: faces of the American Century, harassed and half-dehumanized, scoffing or debauched: so purposeless, unusable and useless faces, yet so smug, so self-satisfied yet so abject—for complacency struggles strangely there with guilt. Faces full of such an immense irresponsibility toward themselves that they tell how high the human cost of our marvelous technological achievements has really been.

Faces to destroy the faith that a man's chief duty in the world is to make himself as comfortable as possible in it, stay comfortable as long as possible and pop off at last, as comfortably as possible.

The faith that the good life means coming into the

world with a Ford in one's future and leaving it at last with a Nash in one's past. That success is a TV aerial on the roof, a faithful wife in the kitchen and a deep freeze in the cellar wherein she may keep his useless memory ever-fresh.

(Let me hurriedly interpose that I am not opposed to TV, Fords, Nashes, refrigerators, nor fidelity. I favor all mechanical improvements about the modern American home. I wish only to voice a suspicion that a house full of functional goodies, and all in good working order at that, does not of itself tote up to happiness.)

Do American faces so often look so lost because they are most tragically trapped between a very real dread of coming alive to something more than merely existing, and an equal dread of going down to the grave without having done more than merely be comfortable?

If so, this is the truly American disease. And would account in part for the fact that we lead the world today in insanity, criminality, alcoholism, narcoticism, psychoanalysm, cancer, homicide and perversion in sex as well as in perversion just for the pure hell of the thing.

Never on the earth of man has he lived so tidily as here amidst such psychological disorder. Never has any people lived so hygienically while daily dousing itself with the ritual slops of guilt. Nowhere has any people set itself a moral code so rigid while applying it quite so flexibly. Never has any people possessed such a superfluity of physical luxuries companioned by such a dearth of emotional necessities.

In no other country is such great wealth, acquired so purposefully, put to such small purpose. Never has any people driven itself so resolutely toward such diverse goals, to derive so little satisfaction from attainment of any. Never has any people been so outwardly confident that God is on its side while being so inwardly terrified lest he be not.

Never has any people endured its own tragedy with so little sense of the tragic.

"I say," Walt Whitman prophesied, "we had best look our times and lands searchingly in the face, like a physician diagnosing some deep disease. Never was there, perhaps, more hollowness at heart than at present, and here in the United States.... It is as if we were somehow being endow'd with a vast and more and more thoroughly appointed body, and then left with little or no soul."[61]

Our assumption of happiness through mechanical ingenuity is nonetheless tragic for being naive. For the bulletins are as false as Mr. Whittaker Chambers, hand over heart, confessing, "I never inform on anyone but I feel something die inside me"—and in the same dying breath murmuring, "Thank you," for $75,000 in magazine serial rights. To see life steadily, and see it whole, as a creature of the deep sees it, from below.

Our myths are so many, our vision so dim, our self-deception so deep and our smugness so gross that scarcely any way now remains of reporting the American Century except from behind the billboards.

"Whin business gits above sellin' ten-pinny nails in a brown-paper cornucopy," Mr. Dooley decided, "'tis hard to tell it from murther."[62]

But behind Business's billboards and Business's headlines and Business's pulpits and Business's press and Business's arsenals, behind the car ads and the subtitles and the commercials, the people of Dickens and Dostoevsky yet endure.

The lost and the overburdened who have to meet life so head-on that they cannot afford either the tweeds that make such a strong impression in certain business circles or the deodorant that does almost as much for one socially. The lost and the overburdened too lost and too overburdened to spare the price of the shaving lotion that automatically initiates one into the fast international set.

It is there that the people of Dickens and Dostoevsky are still torn by the paradox of their own humanity; yet endure the ancestral problems of the heart in conflict with itself. Theirs are still the defeats in which everything is lost, theirs victories that fall close enough to the heart to afford living hope. Whose defeats cost everything of real value. Whose grief grieves on universal bones.

And it is there the young man or woman seeking to report the American century seriously must seek, if it is the truth he seeks.

say we had best look our times and lands searchingly in the face,
like a physician diagnosing some deep disease. Never was there, per-
haps, more hollowness at heart than at present, and here in the
United States. Genuine belief seems to have left us. The underlying
principles of the States are not honestly believ'd in (for all this hectic
glow, and these melodramatic screamings), nor is humanity itself
believ'd in. What penetrating eye does not everywhere see through the
mask? The spectacle is appalling. We live in an atmosphere of
hypocrisy throughout. The men believe not in the women, nor the
women in the men. A scornful superciliousness rules in literature. The
aim of all the littérateurs *is to find something to make fun of. A lot*
of churches, sects, etc., the most dismal phantasms I know, usurp the
name of religion. Conversation is a mass of badinage. From deceit in
the spirit, the mother of all false deeds, the offspring is already incal-
culable. An acute and candid person, in the revenue department in
Washington, who is led by the course of his employment to regularly
visit the cities, north, south, and west, to investigate frauds, has
talked much with me about his discoveries. The depravity of the busi-
ness classes of our country is not less than has been supposed, but infi-
nitely greater. The official services of America, national, state, and

municipal, in all their branches and departments, except the judicia-ry, are saturated in corruption, bribery, falsehood, maladministra-tion; and the judiciary is tainted. The great cities reek with respectable as much as non-respectable robbery and scoundrelism. In fashionable life, flippancy, tepid amours, weak infidelism, small aims, or no aims at all, only to kill time. In business (this all-devour-ing modern word, business), the one sole object is, by any means, pecuniary gain. The magician's serpent in the fable ate up all the other serpents; and moneymaking is our magician's serpent, remain-ing today sole master of the field. The best class we show is but a mob of fashionably dressed speculators and vulgarians. True, indeed, behind this fantastic farce, enacted on the visible stage of society, solid things and stupendous labors are to be discovered, existing crudely and going on in the background, to advance and tell themselves in time. Yet the truths are none the less terrible. I say that our New World democracy, however great a success in uplifting the masses out of their sloughs, in materialistic development, products, and in a cer-tain highly deceptive superficial popular intellectuality, is, so far, an almost complete failure in its social aspects, and in really grand reli-gious, moral, literary and aesthetic results. In vain do we march with

unprecedented strides to empire so colossal, outvying the antique,
beyond Alexander's, beyond the proudest sway of Rome. In vain have
we annexed Texas, California, Alaska, and reach north for Canada
and south for Cuba. It is as if we were somehow being endow'd with
a vast and more and more thoroughly appointed body, and then left
with little or no soul.

—Walt Whitman,
from *Democratic Vistas*
1871[63]

A F T E R W O R D

NELSON ALGREN'S WRITING METHod relied on accretion. He returned, year after year, to given situations and characters, building up the surface almost more like a painter than a writer, until he found the emotion he wanted. When he was writing *The Man with the Golden Arm*, through a dozen drafts in some places and "forty rewritings that still aren't right"[64] in others, the drug addiction of the drum-playing card dealer Frankie Machine didn't enter in until nearly the very end. It was a wholly new element through which Algren gave the book, along with its title and narrative thrust, a different feeling— not the war now but the war's aftermath, its unendingness. "I was going to write a war novel," Algren would tell Alston Anderson and Terry Southern in a *Paris Review* interview in 1955, "but it turned out to be this *Golden Arm* thing. I mean, the war kind of slipped away, and those people with the hypos came along and that was it,"[65] speaking as if the composition of his finest novel relied on a chain of events, this process of layering, really as outside his control as if he were describing changes in the weather.

Algren's earliest published story began as a letter home. He was encouraged by an acquaintance to recast it as fiction and submit it to *Story* magazine; it was accepted, and that led to a contract for his first novel. Algren's second novel, *Never Come Morning*, is a retelling of an early story called "A Bottle of Milk for Mother." The last novel published in his lifetime, *A Walk on the Wild Side*, is a rewrite of his first novel, *Somebody in Boots*. Characters and situations recur from book to book—the police lineup is the classic example—with new layers of meaning and emotion.

Nonconformity was the result of a layering process roughly the reverse of the one that produced *Man with the Golden Arm*. In the beginning was the story of what Algren saw as his humiliation in Hollywood after a movie producer purchased the rights to *Golden Arm* and brought Algren to the coast to write the screenplay. Included here as an appendix, Algren's sardonic account is his starting point, almost in the same way Frankie Machine's habit was *Golden Arm*'s ending point. He then adds layers, most importantly that of F. Scott Fitzgerald's autobiographical account of his nervous breakdown, as described in *The Crack-Up*. Algren keeps adding to the surface of his canvas, layer by layer, alternating the high with the low, giving glimpses of a moral universe in the most unexpected venues, scouring books and magazines for *sententiae* to shore up his arguments. Just as *Golden Arm*, through layering, became a text about the unendingness of an internalized state of war, this essay was transformed into a text about the responsibilities writers carry with them, about the unendingness, as it were, of the writer's art. Through this startling metamorphosis, in which Algren lets his writing carry him from a state of utter self-absorption to one where the subject is in the end no longer himself at all (from a text about "my war with the United States as represented by Kim Novak"[66] to an essay that affirms the power writers wield when they resist the status quo), the nexus of the essay remains the bond he feels with Fitzgerald. From this link, the real subject of the essay emerges, which is the debt owed by writers to the lives they write about.

Since Fitzgerald is known for imagining the very rich and Algren for writing about the poor, the two aren't usually mentioned in the same breath. But in *Nonconformity* Algren cites Fitzgerald and Fitzgerald alone as father of the school to which he belongs. This is no longer the Proletarian school to which Algren had been linked by academics. Precisely *because* their subjects are so different, it is a tempting—and powerful—alternative way of reading that he is proposing. What is important about Fitzgerald, Algren is saying here, is that he put himself at the service of the characters he wrote about. And perhaps without fully realizing it, Algren is describing himself as well, since this is precisely the point that has been made over the years by the few critics writing astutely about him.[67]

Algren is achieving something approaching self-awareness through his empathy with Fitzgerald, at the same time as he is also attempting to seek a higher appreciation for the kind of writing they both do. The "I" of the first section (now the appendix) is transmuted into the "he," the nonconforming writer, of the body of the essay. Quoting long passages from many of the most radical defendants of free speech of the last hundred years—Whitman, Twain, Faulkner, Learned Hand, de Beauvoir (and not forgetting Mr. Martin Dooley, barkeep, and Leo Durocher, utility infielder)—Algren seeks to replace the image of the defeated writer with which he began with that of a writer-archetype whose profession as guardian of certain necessary truths is unimpeachable, and who has a role to play in society as basic and essential as that of the policeman, the judge or the teacher, although different from each of these.

Nonconformity was written between 1950 and 1953. In the arc of Algren's life, this period was the absolute high point: *The Man with the Golden Arm*, published to near-universal acclaim, had won the first National Book Award; in March 1950 Algren flew to New York to receive the award at a black-tie ceremony from Eleanor Roosevelt herself. His fans included Hemingway and the esteemed critic Malcolm Cowley. Hollywood agent Irving Lazar was wooing him and movie idol John Garfield wanted to star as Frankie Machine, the young man at the heart of *Golden Arm* struggling under all the trouble in the world.

In his personal life there was also a fullness—or at least the possibility of a fullness—that Algren had come to know only recently. Simone de Beauvoir had called him out of the blue in February 1947, on the recommendation of a mutual friend. They had begun an affair that developed into the most passionate attachment either of them had ever known. While by the early 1950s the distance between them had grown, Algren was unable to give up on this once-in-a-lifetime attachment to a woman who was both an intellectual equal and a writer with aspirations every bit as large as his own; his hope was that she might yet leave Sartre for him. Thus it was that after the success of *The Man with the Golden Arm*, there was a short-lived period of enormous self-confidence for Algren. He was famous, sought after, in love and, still in his early forties, looking forward to a long career among the first circle of novelists.

It must have struck him as strange that at the very moment when his work was breaking through, the society at large seemed to be changing from an open to a closed one. In her biography of Algren, Bettina Drew writes that the "growing atmosphere of conformity and distress" may have changed Algren's writing plans. And indeed, the jailing of the Hollywood Ten in 1950 cast a pall over the efforts of those who, like Algren, saw themselves as voices the government would like to see silenced. The same year, the Senate approved legislation permitting executions for peacetime spying and passed the Internal Security Act, which called for concentration camp detention for people with radical ideas. Also that year, MacArthur's aggressive response in Korea had brought U.S. troops so deeply into North Korea that they seemed to be threatening Chinese soil, and the world faced the possibility of an atomic conflict if Russia came to the support of the Chinese.

Algren was, both publicly and privately, to borrow Sartre's expression, an *engaged* writer, having participated in left-leaning organizations since the late 1930s, and doing so with increasing visibility by 1950. On January 15, 1951, along with Arthur Miller and 15 others, he signed a letter placed as an ad in *The New York Times* admonishing people to "Speak up for freedom!" In 1952 Algren became the honorary chairman of the Chicago Committee to Secure Justice in the Rosenberg Case, which catapulted him high on the FBI's list of suspected Communists and infuriated J. Edgar Hoover. In part inspired by the example of European intellectuals like Sartre and de Beauvoir, Algren's sense of his civic duties became more acute. In particular, the anti-Semitism and pressure to conform he saw behind the demonizing of Ethel and Julius Rosenberg concerned him. In March 1952 he referred to them as "a man and woman being put to death for nonconformity."[68]

It is in this context that we can appreciate the large ambition which informs *Nonconformity*. Algren wrote this essay at a moment when he knew his words carried weight. He had never before, and would never again, attempt to address the public directly in this way, eschewing the cloak of the novelist. To do so required that he overcome a host of self-protective habits. *Nonconformity* was written to open people's eyes to the dangers, especially to writers, that Algren saw all around in the era of Joe McCarthy. Just like each of his novels—and this is one of Algren's great strengths— *Nonconformity* describes a particular historical moment. Differently from any other book he wrote, the moment in question here—"between the H Bomb and the A" he calls it repeatedly in the essay, between one act of inhumanity and the prospect of a much greater one—was being exploited by certain groups in the government to silence people, and especially creative artists. So the temptation for Algren to speak to and of this historical moment directly and in his own voice, rather than through a novel, became irresistible. In an age when the pressure to hide—and conformity is precisely concealment and then the effects of that concealment—had become so great, Algren felt compelled to come out of hiding, to express his convictions bluntly, to connect his private credo with his public persona and to do so not just in a speech, interview or letter, but in a full-fledged book-length work of literature.

In the past Algren had usually set himself apart from the risk-takers. A few years earlier, when urged to join the Lincoln Brigade on the way to fight for freedom and the Spanish Republic, he had unhesitatingly refused. As he told H. E. F. Donohue: "I didn't go to the war in Spain, although I was asked. It was assumed that I would go. My defense when asked why aren't you there was that I don't want to get killed."[69]

But now he felt a new confidence in his own voice. And while it is entirely conjecture to say so, perhaps he felt he had to best Sartre in some kind of imagined battle for Simone's heart. Whatever the reason, this essay represented a new kind of writing for Algren.

Writing about Algren for the *Village Voice* in 1985, Tom Carson described him as "one of the few American writers, increasingly uncommon since Dreiser, in whom compassion for the dispossessed does not involve a sort of mental portage to reach them." Carson continues, "The great revelation for him had been that deprivation was not an abnormal social category but a human absolute, and the pressure... comes from a writer trying to measure up to the people he's writing about."[70] There was something in the way Algren treated the characters who inhabited his novels and stories, something that lent them, as Studs Terkel says, their "respectability." Algren refused to draw a line between him and them, between us and them. Carson has it right: Algren faces the reader with the paradox of a writer trying to *measure up* to the miserable lives of his characters. Here was the essential human dilemma with which both Fitzgerald and Algren struggled. It perplexed Fitzgerald and left him distraught; he saw the struggle as a fatal weakness, one that threatened his ability to survive as both a writer and a human being. To Algren it was an essential strength, and more than anything else, the quality that defined his work. He saw himself in a profound sense in the service of his material. And he considered his material not as a narrow stripe but as a broad swath, a representative sampling, of humanity. He felt his characters resonated with universal truths. "There is no such thing as a normal life," Algren would say to H. E. F. Donohue. "It's never lived that way."[71] And no one else but Algren could write, as he did in November 1962 in a new preface to his 1942 novel *Never Come Morning*, "The source of the criminal act, I believed twenty years ago and believe yet, is not in the criminal but in the righteous man."[72]

There is a line in the poem with which Algren closed his 1973 fiction and nonfiction collection, *The Last Carousel*, that codifies the enigma of his writing credo: "All those whose lives were lived by someone else." The catalyst for his novel *Never Come Morning* had been newspaper accounts of a nineteen-year-old murderer named Bernard Sawicki who was quoted on the day of his arrest saying he "never expected to be twenty-one anyway," virtually the same words Algren has spoken by Bruno "Lefty" Bicek in the novel. And on the day of his sentencing to death, Sawicki told the judge, "The hell with you, I can take it."[73] These are Algren's people, the objects of what James Giles[74] calls his "harsh compassion," those who don't get to live their lives. Algren's friend, the photographer Art Shay, remembers Algren reading in the newspaper about the murder of an entire family by someone they had picked up hitchhiking. Algren scrutinized the pictures accompanying the newspaper story, including one of the murderer, who had "HARD LUCK" tattooed across his knuckles. "That poor sonofabitch," Algren commented. He was referring to the murderer. "My wife wanted to throw [Algren] out," Shay remembered, adding: "Nelson's humanity. He could see what could drive a man to something like that. Only Jesus Christ... could have that kind of attitude."[75]

And yet, the emotional life of Bruno "Lefty" Bicek in the novel is finally completely his own and not Bernard Sawicki's at all. Algren's characters were always different from the people whose words and actions inspired them. He borrowed figures of speech and other details as they suited him, but the tragicomic moral universe of Algren's novels is finally all his own. And this puts another spin on the line in the poem. Not unlike the people who inhabit his novels, Algren was so consumed by the lives he wrote about that he too, like Fitzgerald, saw his life being lived by others.

As a society we hope to be judged by the achievements of our best and brightest; individually we may wish to express our finest qualities in what we do. Algren reminds us that self-knowledge will not come by either of those routes. He believed that we can't know ourselves except by looking deeply into the eyes and hearts of our most forlorn, most broken-down, who are shorn of all but their essential human qualities, and sometimes even of those. Only by looking there will we be able to see into ourselves. (The last line of the poem quoted above is "Within a rain that lightly rains regret.") He wrote about them with unparalleled beauty, writing gorgeously of hard luck cases of all kinds—as if that were the only thing worth writing about. He was not the first of his kind. Yet no other writer of his generation had Algren's blend of radicalism with a vision that was so personal and lyrical.

There has been surprisingly little serious critical attention paid to Nelson Algren's writing since his death in 1981. One valiant and thorough popular biography by Bettina Drew. One excellent scholarly monograph by James Giles. And that's about it. Amazingly little, considering that Algren's novels themselves continue to be widely read and studied, that Algren himself is considered by many to be among the handful of great American novelists of the 20th century, and that no one has yet made him known to us in the way that other writers of his stature have been made known— weighed and measured, analyzed and interpreted, and in this way inducted into the pantheon of American literature.

It is almost as if Algren were someone we don't want to know. Someone to be respected, but not included. A writer who somehow slipped past those who stand as our nation's self-appointed literary gatekeepers, rather than being accepted by them. He is still the quintessential out-sider. Unlike the writings of, say, Faulkner or Hemingway, Algren's works comprise a literary backwater, known to many but visited with understanding by few. For most read-ers, his world is a landscape we lack either the words or the desire to find familiar.

Like Fitzgerald, he published his first novel in his early twenties, but unlike Fitzgerald, Algren did not suc-cumb to weaknesses of spirit and misfortunes of circum-stance. At the time he wrote *Nonconformity* he had been a practicing writer of fiction for twenty years. After *Nonconformity* he would go on writing books for another thirty years—until the end of his life at the not-unripe age of 72. There is a completeness to his artistic output—four major novels, a half-dozen other books of lasting impor-tance written over a span of fifty years—that saves him from the sense of doom that has engulfed so many other American writers in this century. Algren is not a tragic fig-ure in the way that Fitzgerald is.

He began as a Proletarian novelist, a member of the John Reed Club, a contributor to Jack Conroy's *Anvil* and the Canadian *Masses*, who wrote with the belief that the dis-enfranchisement of the Depression was going to turn our society on its head. Twenty years later his vision had taken on greater complexity and depth. Along with the things he'd always known to be true, his personal journey had taught him much that gave his mature output broader definition.

Nonconformity and *The Man with the Golden Arm* are the work of a different writer from the one who penned *Somebody in Boots*. He had learned a different faith, and a willingness to continue wrestling with the world whether or not he was able to change it. Alongside his apparent tragic vision, there is in Algren by this point, as in Beckett, a corresponding non-tragic one.

Into this literary situation, *Nonconformity* lands with a very specific and relevant history and much to say about Algren, in his own words, that was not generally known. It shows him as isolated, and as self-isolating. Indeed, his subject in *Nonconformity* emphatically is not the importance of solidarity among living writers. He cruelly attacks James T. Farrell, and jabs at other lesser lights of his epoch. And the name of the one writer with whom Algren had had the closest and most mutually supportive relationship, Richard Wright, comes up only once in passing. The enthusiastic reception Wright's *Native Son* (1940) received on publication had fueled Algren's faith that his own work would be appreciated, and Wright had written the introduction to *Never Come Morning*. But by 1952, the emotion Algren attached to his connection with Wright belonged to a different decade.

Nonconformity nonetheless shows Algren to be much more thoughtful, literate and "literary" than the image he cultivated over the years of someone who, when he wasn't writing novels, was playing cards, betting on horses, or socializing with killers and drug addicts. He did all that. At the same time, as he shows here, he took the responsibility of the writer in deadly earnest, and could examine the history of free expression not just in terms of the immediate crisis of McCarthyism he was facing in 1952, but as a centuries-long struggle.

In *Nonconformity*, Algren turned to subject matter that was, for him, quite banal—himself, other writers, the writing art, the responsibility of the intellectual, the dangers of conformity for those who create. This once in his life he chose to write at length about the state of literature because he felt that suddenly something was happening to our nation to cause artistic creation generally, and his own artistic output in particular, to be under an extraordinary threat.

Sadly, after completing *The Man with the Golden Arm,* Algren did not publish another novel for seven years, and then abandoned the novel altogether for two decades, although he wrote many more books.[76] His decade of unabated achievement had been as amazingly fertile as anything in the history of American literature. It had generated, in chronological order, *Never Come Morning; Neon Wilderness,* his now-classic story collection; *The Man with the Golden Arm; Chicago: City on the Make,* his prose-poem paean to Chicago; and *Nonconformity: Writing on Writing,* five very different major works of the imagination, each an enduring work. None were written easily, and by the end he had spent himself. The self-assurance he felt by 1949-50, and still had in 1952, progressively dissolved thereafter into an anguished battle between his compassion and a new-found bitterness and cynicism. *Nonconformity*, which he wrote in defiance of an era, was also a plea to himself to persist in the face of increasing opposition from within, opposition based in his own mounting loss of faith that his writing was truly valued. And in the end Algren's own life would share something of the aimlessness and pathos of his characters.

Algren offers up an unbroken line of assenting voices in *Nonconformity* to bolster his point of view, and then, with his novelist's instinct, breaks that line with the Fitzgerald figure, returning the whole to the very real dilemma from which he could not separate himself. Twain, Conrad, Faulkner, de Beauvoir, Whitman—all come across as winners, men and women who run no risk of conforming, no risk either of going hungry or being forgotten. Not so Fitzgerald. He is the writer Algren feels most passionate about, but he is also the one whose presence in the essay never stops troubling Algren. Fitzgerald is shown as having given too much, one for whom the price had been too great, one who became the victim of his own gift. And Algren has too much respect for Fitzgerald to try to unravel that knot, so that while the essay goes further, Fitzgerald's price, like K.'s in Kafka's novel—which he also quotes—is not forgotten and in the end saves the essay, with irony and weariness, from mere optimism.

A decade after writing *Nonconformity*, Algren had not forgotten about it. He lent a version of the manuscript, now ironically titled "Things of the Earth: A Groundhog's View," to H. E. F. Donohue, who was interviewing him for the book that would become *Conversations with Nelson Algren*, and Donohue questioned him about the essay at great length. At first Algren's answers center on the importance of "working out of straight compassion." Then he brings up anger: "Nobody who is really angry goes around being angry," he tells Donohue. Algren next begins to talk about the writer's compulsion: "There were things [writers like Hemingway and Faulkner] had to do for their own survival... it had to be total.... It goes all the way."[77] The battle is never-ending and never won.

Coming several years after Sartre's *What Is Literature?* (1947), in which the Frenchman first introduced the idea of the *engaged* writer as a philosophical essence, and several years before Robert Frank's *The Americans* (1956), in which the reality Algren is fighting against in *Nonconformity* could already be described lushly, elegiacally, as part of a world breathing its last, Algren's essay had a sociological urgency when it was written. For us today, it is a powerful expression of optimism, of hope, by a great talent who within a few years and then for the rest of his life would be without the ebullience and earnestness he shows here in such abundance. There is a great ocean of feeling in this essay; and it is important for us to remember that that precious commodity is not something to be taken for granted. So many American writers of this century have given in, one way or another; and their lives inhabit Algren's essay, since it is a plea to writers not to give in. Along with its many assertions of the strength of writers, it also speaks of their vulnerability. *Nonconformity* reminds us of the essential truth that people whose faith in humanity is most forceful are often also those in whom it is most evanescent.

Ultimately Algren, like his early contemporary John Steinbeck, would lose his faith that the American reading public considered his books to be important. And yet, as Kurt Vonnegut recently reminded me, that loss of faith was pure paranoia on the part of both men. Their work is appreciated. And in its own way their public has never stopped telling them so.

Daniel Simon
New York
April 1996

Historical Note and Acknowledgements

SOMETIME IN MAY 1956 NELSON Algren called up Van Allen Bradley, then literary editor of the *Chicago Daily News,* and invited him to a drinking session at Riccardo's, a dark and respectable restaurant that was one of Algren's favorite haunts. At the appointed hour Algren showed up with his ex-wife Amanda, who had recently come back into his life, and the occasion turned out to have a double edge. First, Algren announced that he had bought Amanda an engagement ring, which he showed off, "proudly and rather schoolboyishly" in Bradley's telling. Algren then produced, and here was the other purpose of the evening, the sole remaining carbon of this essay, and dictated to Bradley the following few words:

"The original of this essay on nonconformity was apparently lost in the mails. This carbon is all that's left."[78]

Thereupon Algren signed and dated the statement and gave it to Bradley along with the manuscript carbon, which Bradley had earlier requested as a souvenir. Algren had chosen to celebrate his decision to remarry Amanda and at the same time to close the door on publishing this essay by giving away his only copy. The two decisions together expressed a loss of innocence for Algren, giving the celebration that night an ironic flavor. He found himself walking backwards into a past marriage without deep attachment and resigning himself to never seeing in print a long piece of writing on which he had been working for several years. There would no longer be any question of marrying Simone de Beauvoir—who had signaled the end of their long and intense affair by moving on to other lovers—or publishing this book, conceived and written during the time of his passion for Simone. Bradley would later refer to the evening at Riccardo's as the dramatic end to "a unique episode in Nelson Algren's career in which I had a share."[79] But it is possible that Bradley didn't grasp the real emotional depths of the drama he had witnessed.

The publication history of *Nonconformity* had begun, as recounted by Bradley, four years earlier on "a summer afternoon in 1952," when he asked Algren to do a piece for the Christmas book section of the *Chicago Daily News*. Algren delivered a short piece, about 2,000 words, adapted from the 20,000-word essay he had been writing on and off for a year or so. Although what Algren gave him was different from what he had asked for, Bradley published it, under the headline "Great Writing Bogged Down in Fear, Says Novelist Algren."[80] As Bradley remembers, "It was a strong and moving indictment, honestly written, and I printed it, expecting a reader controversy to break over my head. It never came. Instead there came an outpouring of applause that amazed us all." Bradley goes on to recount how "the head of the Department of Religion at a famous Catholic college used it as a sermon text, as did an Episcopal minister in Mississippi." One reader ordered a hundred copies to use as a Christmas greeting. *The Nation* "asked, and received, the right to reprint the article, as did other publications."[81]

A Chicago publisher offered to bring it out as a book. Then Doubleday, which had published Algren's last novel, *The Man with the Golden Arm,* insisted on publishing the essay. At that point, in Bradley's account, Algren "began to rewrite, enlarging the essay with fresh thoughts and with extracts from a lecture he had given at the University of Missouri."[82]

In early March 1953, as recounted in Drew's biography, Algren's passport application was denied. "It has been alleged that you were a Communist," he was informed by the passport office. In April, as part of an ongoing FBI investigation, two informants "of known reliability" gave evidence that Algren had been a Party member in the late thirties. In June another informant produced a 1937 letter from Algren allegedly proving that he'd been a Communist.[83] In early June Doubleday was still preparing to publish the book, and Algren sent them the reworked manuscript with their preferred title, "The State of Literature." In addition to Bradley's prefatory note, they had commissioned an introduction from the esteemed literary critic Maxwell Geismar, who had done the best scholarly writing on Algren to date. On June 3, 1953, Geismar wrote to Algren, "This will be one of the first books they will burn: congratulations."[84]

That month Julius and Ethel Rosenberg were electrocuted, affecting Algren deeply. His letters to de Beauvoir become importunate, including descriptions of the horror of marriage without love. He plowed through the English translation of her *The Second Sex* and listed his phone in her name. By August, Doubleday had decided the book needed further changes and sent an editor all the way from New York to assist Algren at his home. "Polishing is a polite phrase you may have run [into]," Algren wrote to Geismar, "and it means polishing a passage until it is polished away. Well, we polished here and we polished there, and every time we polished one into oblivion I had a fresh rough-hewn zircon to insert."[85]

In September Doubleday indeed refused to publish and forfeited the small sum of money ($1,500) they had paid in advance. As Bradley tells it, Doubleday "decided NOT to publish the book (which deals with nonconformity), and I accused them of being afraid of McCarthy (Senator Joe) and others of his ilk; Doubleday denied this...." Algren wrote to Geismar, "I put too much work in it not to feel disappointed as hell. But I'm still in the land of the living at least, and that's a little something."[86] He sent it on to his agent at the time, Madeleine Brennan, with the understanding that she would seek another publisher for it. She either lost it or never received it. There Algren let the matter rest, in an act of resignation reminiscent of Mark Twain who, after writing his anti-war manifesto, *The War Prayer,* said, "I have told the whole truth in that, and only dead men can tell the truth in this world. It can be published after I am dead."[87]

Bradley's prefatory note (written at Doubleday's request in 1953, while Algren was still working on the original essay), Algren's two-sentence *envoi* from that May of 1956, along with Bradley's memo on the whole affair, various copies of the shorter adaptations published in the *Chicago Daily News, The Nation* and elsewhere, and the carbon of the essay itself—all found their way into the Algren archive at the Ohio State University Library in Columbus a few years later, where they lay untouched for another quarter-century.[88] In November 1986 I found them at OSU among Algren's other papers. I was not the only one to notice them. Bettina Drew, Algren's biographer, came across the essay a few months before I did; others may have noticed it too. I felt strongly, as I read it for the first time that November, that even a generation later than originally planned , it still demanded to be published.

Nonconformity is not like any other literary essay, and perhaps for that reason, even now, it is not an easy book to read. For the last ten years I've wrestled with it and tried to understand it. Since it is a very short book, people have occasionally asked me what's taking so long, and I've said that researching Algren's quotes takes time. But that is only partly true. The rest of the answer is that trying to understand what Algren means here takes time: what he means when he describes the particular responsibility of writers, or the addict's "special grace," or what he calls "the American disease"—our blindness to our own pathos—or national characteristics he thought were common to writers and criminals, including the need to get back at society.

I believe *Nonconformity* to be Algren's credo, and at the same time an expression of profound crisis within Algren. And I believe *Nonconformity* is one of the strangest, toughest and truest essays in the history of American letters, linking high and low as they have not been linked before or since, rendering a harmony to the whole that was new on this earth when Algren created it. I can think of no other literary work that resists and then yields its meanings so powerfully.

Nonconformity in manuscript form presented my associate C. S. O'Brien and me with a dilemma. It was clearly a major find: a book-length treatise on the writing art, from the period of Algren's finest work. On the other hand, the essay was unpublishable as it stood: a mess of impossibly long quotes by others interrupted its flow; Algren's own words often read too much like a notebook, too little like an essay; its passion itself also made it seem unlike an essay. To simply publish it in the form in which I'd found it would have been no service to Algren or his readers. To bring it into publishable shape would be difficult, but it was the only choice other than not to publish it at all.

Given my conviction that *Nonconformity* represented a major effort on Algren's part, I did not want to bring it out without verifying his quotes—a major stumbling block as none were referenced. In some cases he indicated his source, in some cases not. I could not publish it as a *fond du tiroir*, a tidbit of no importance left behind in his desk drawer. If it were to be published at all, every possible quote and reference would have to be verified.

That work, although time-consuming, turned out to be both possible and gratifying. Generally a quoted author could be identified, either because Algren indeed named him or her, or from the context of the quotation. In some cases our starting point was nothing more than a gut feeling that the source might be this writer or that one, because it sounded American, French or Russian, 20th century or 19th. Most often Algren chose from books popular at the time he was writing. Once a particular author was identified, O'Brien and I would check which books by that author had been released between 1947 and 1953. In the case of Simone de Beauvoir, for example, that narrowed it down to two English translations of her work, *America Day by Day*, published in England in 1952, and *The Second Sex*, published in America in 1953. De Beauvoir never quite believed that Algren really read the whole 750-page *Second Sex*, as he told her he had, but we gave him the benefit of the doubt. We found several of the de Beauvoir quotes easily in *America Day by Day*, and one day, on my third or fourth assault, after nearly giving up, the last quote from *Nonconformity* stared back at me from near the end of *The Second Sex*.

Of the ninety-odd endnotes we have appended to *Nonconformity*, nearly all were the product of investigations of various degrees of absurdity by myself or O'Brien. I'd reached the point of unquiet desperation after skimming all Dostoevsky's major novels, again and again, without locating the long passage Algren quotes, when O'Brien showed up one day with Dostoevsky's obscure, 1,100-page, autobiographical *The Diary of a Writer;* there, the next day, on page 7, I found my quote. We spent untold hours rereading Shakespeare, among others, in an effort to place a suspicious rhyming couplet. We never found it anywhere and in the end I deleted it from the text, with some trepidation, but correctly I think.

I had heard about a speech by the great jurist Learned Hand that had been reprinted in the *Saturday Review* in November 1952, just when Algren would have been working on the essay. I went to the text of that speech, which was widely discussed at the time, and found the exact source of the long passage Algren quoted from Hand.

As O'Brien and I began to find the quotes, one by one, we discovered that Algren was rarely letter perfect. Even his favorite quotes tended to be slight misquotes. As the passing months turned into years, I developed a pet theory. It is that Algren must have had an extremely good memory, nearly eidetic, or photographic, in fact. So many of his quotes were near perfect, but a little off here or there; it seemed that, at least in some cases, he must have been going from memory. Had he been copying from a text as he was looking at it, the errors would have been more of a typographical nature, whereas in fact his misquotes were more often creative rewrites. He had a peculiar way of making sure his sources came out speaking Algrenese.

Part of our work entailed restoring the correct wording where possible. For example, Algren has F. Scott Fitzgerald asking, "Why was I identified with the very objects of my horror and compassion?" But this is more shorthand than quotation. Fitzgerald actually wrote, "I only wanted absolute quiet to think out why I had developed a sad attitude toward sadness, a melancholy attitude toward melancholy and a tragic attitude toward tragedy—why I had become identified with the objects of my horror or compassion." I emended Algren's version so that it now reads, "I only wanted absolute quiet to think out... why I had become identified with the objects of my horror or compassion." And the full text of the passage is given in an endnote. In our finished version there is, as I believe there should be, more of a mingling of distinct voices than there was in the manuscript, and only Algren now speaks pure Algrenese.

There were, however, exceptions to this rule. The majority of the quotes we were able to track down were restored to their original form, as in the case of the Fitzgerald passage noted above. But sometimes I came across source material that seemed to carry the same idea as what Algren had put between quotes, but without Algren's scent on it. A few of these I left in Algren's words, in effect misquoting, and supplied the original text in an endnote, since in these passages, knowingly or unknowingly, Algren seemed to have made the text his own. In these cases I couldn't simply restore the passage without taking something away from what he'd written. In one such example he quotes de Beauvoir this way: "It isn't that young Americans don't wish to do great things, but that they don't know there are great things to be done." She had written something along the same line, which in the English translation read: "Ambitions for greatness are often the source of many deceptions, and indicted by faults Americans do not know.... In order to lose themselves in the pursuit of an object, they find themselves without an object at all." To have restored her wording in this case would have been to change his meaning.

If his near-perfect memory was a curse of sorts for us, another habit that became apparent was a blessing. I noticed that very often Algren would quote from either the beginning or the end of a book; in our research this was a tic of his for which we were grateful, since we could sometimes find what we were looking for soon after we'd located the right volume. I am sure that Algren read novels he liked from cover to cover, but I have come to believe that when it came to works of nonfiction, his mind was so sure of itself, his curiosity so absorbed in the things of the real world and his own perception of them, that he rarely read non-fiction books to the end, with the possible exception of de Beauvoir's *The Second Sex,* where his broken heart may have forced the issue.

Algren was a novelist with training as a journalist, not a scholar or essayist, and he wasn't adept at weaving quotes into the stream of his own thought. And yet the abundant quotes in *Nonconformity* were well chosen and are essential to the effectiveness of the essay; they served, and served well, as a kind of chorus of assenting voices speaking to an historical moment, when elsewhere the loudest noise-makers, like Senator Joe McCarthy, were drowning out such voices. I had neither the desire nor the right to edit them out, but could not in good conscience simply leave them in either. I chose to resolve the issue by dividing the essay into sections, into which it fell naturally and to good effect, to reduce within each section any unacceptably long quotes, and then to present between the sections the full and accurate quote in its entirety. In this way the body of the essay could be professionally edited as it would have been were Algren still alive, and the quotes could be saved as interludes intersplicing his text.

In two cases, the new format required long quotations where Algren had none, and I chose passages that would not have been appropriate had the essay been published in 1953, as Algren had intended. One is de Beauvoir's description of her first meeting Algren in 1947, the second is Algren's answer to the question "What is American literature?" taken from H. E. F. Donohue's *Conversations with Nelson Algren.* Since the essay is seeing its first publication only now, nearly half a century later, I believe both these additions are fitting.

The archive held two slightly variant typescripts of almost the same length, which were largely identical. They must have been roughly contemporaneous, and the discrepancy was probably the result of final retyping in June 1953. There was no way of telling which of the two came later, and even had I been able to tell, this alone would not have been decisive; the later version might well have reflected Algren's deflated mood at the time, his increasing doubts about Doubleday's commitment, and displayed more second-guessing than improvement. In the end I followed one of the two almost in its entirety, introducing versions of less than identical passages from the other in only a few places where there seemed to be something worth saving that did not appear in both.

Since Algren eventually borrowed his own original title, *A Walk on the Wild Side,* for his 1956 novel, the essay needed to be renamed. I didn't much like Doubleday's choice, "The State of Literature," and neither had Algren. Other titles he came up with over the years tended to be self-mocking, reflecting, I think, his frustration and bitterness over the fact that the book was never published. I chose *Nonconformity* because it was the word by which Algren most often referred to the book, in conversation and in writing, because I like it, and because it hasn't become any less provocative over the years.

With thanks to Robert A. Tibbetts, former Curator of Special Collections at Ohio State University, Columbus, which, along with the Newberry Library in Chicago, holds Algren's papers. Mr. Tibbetts received me warmly when I visited, and with humor and great warmth left me to my devices. Thanks to Stephen Deutch, for his marvelous pictures and who introduced me to Algren's old neighborhood, the first time he had returned there since his friend's death; to Bettina Drew, for keeping the facts of Algren's life and work alive; to James Giles for keeping us thinking about Algren in new ways; to Art Shay, Algren's other photographer-friend, from whose book, *Nelson Algren's Chicago,* came our cover images; and to Studs Terkel, who has also remained Algren's friend all these years. Special thanks to Kurt Vonnegut, who initially challenged the viability of publishing *Nonconformity* at all and then never stopped asking me how work on it was progressing; and to

Victor Navasky for helping sort out several points of fact regarding the period we now call the McCarthy era.

Two writers literally volunteered to work with me, at times when we could not afford to pay them, because of my association with Algren. They are Tom Downs and C. S. O'Brien. O'Brien became my sounding board. It was O'Brien who fought for keeping Algren's opening section (now the appendix) on the basis of its being the nearest parallel to Fitzgerald's *The Crack-Up*. And it was O'Brien as well who tracked down Algren's references to the inimitable Mr. Dooley, a character I had never heard of.

When I first contacted Algren's friend, and still his agent, Candida Donadio, in 1984, I had not yet published a book. And yet her agency, then as now, treated me with the respect they accorded anyone passionate about Algren. Over the years Candida, Ruth Sherman who as Algren's surviving relative is executor of his estate, Eric Ashworth and Neil Olson have been gracious and helpful and always convey to me the palpable sense that Nelson is nearby.

I owe a debt of gratitude to Elinor Nauen for her inspired copyediting of *Nonconformity*; to Cynthia Cameros and Moyra Davey for sharing the journey of the past year at Seven Stories Press, to Brendamichelle Morris for her help securing permissions for *Nonconformity*, and to my wife, Adriana Scopino, without whose help this work could not have been completed.

To H. E. F. Donohue, whose *Conversations with*

Nelson Algren preceded this book and led the way, I am particularly thankful. Every serious reader of Algren knows *Conversations*. In its pages Algren's personality lives like an eternal flame. Several passages from *Conversations* appear in *Nonconformity* because they are illuminations of Algren's work and his spirit. My hope for *Nonconformity* is that it may help readers of Algren continue on that road, in that spirit.

—D. S.

APPENDIX

[*In October 1949, the actor John Garfield decided he'd like to star as Frankie Machine in a movie version of Algren's harsh and brilliant new novel,* The Man with the Golden Arm. *Garfield sent his producer, Bob Roberts, to Chicago, where he struck a deal with the writer. In early 1950 Algren and a friend, an addict named Acker, who Algren thought could serve as a technical adviser on the film, traveled on the stylish Super Chief train to Hollywood. Once there, things got off to a bad start. Garfield only swept in and out between games of tennis; Algren kept talking about renegotiating the deal. Within days communication had broken down to the point where Roberts had Algren served with summonses. Algren felt Hollywood was mistreating him, and it only made sense to him to treat Hollywood with equal scorn and loathing in return. In the end a better deal was struck, and Algren returned to Chicago, somewhat mollified, to work on the screenplay, which he completed in three months. For the next two years, as the pervasive persecution of leftists and liberals intensified and as the number of blacklisted actors, writers and directors increased, the film project foundered. Then, in May 1952, under threat of*

*perjury prosecution for refusing to name Communists by claim-
ing he didn't know any, Garfield, aged 39, died of a sudden
heart attack.*

*Several years later, and after Algren spent another dis-
astrous episode in Hollywood, the film of* The Man with the
Golden Arm *was finally made by Otto Preminger, to Algren's
intense and everlasting dissatisfaction. He would come to refer
to his Hollywood experience as "my war with the United States
as represented by Kim Novak" (who co-starred, alongside Frank
Sinatra). The hurt of it stayed with him, partly because he
made very little money from it, and partly, perhaps, because he
understood it to be emblematic of his larger conflict with the
whole country.*

*Originally, Algren had placed his satiric account of his
Hollywood experience as the opening scene of this essay. Since
both its tone and its substance set it apart from the rest of*
Nonconformity, *it is included here as an appendix, of interest
to the reader of* Nonconformity *as vintage Algren and as what
triggered him to write the book.   —D.S.]*

L ife, Peer Gynt decided, is a matter of passing safe and
dry-shod down the rushing stream of time. When, not
long past, I discovered myself to be passing not only safe
and snugly shod, but downright lavishly set up, I felt,
though there was no Anitra near, that I agreed with Peer at
last. The downright lavish setup was called, exotically
enough, the Garden of Allah.[89] But the only exotic thing
about it was that the rent was free. Free because I was being

accorded the Ten-Day-Hollywood-Hospitality Treatment, an operation predicated upon the assumption that half a grand allotted from a producer's budget toward the comfort and entertainment of any writer from the hinterland is certain, with the help of that Yogi sun, to arouse such slavering gratitude in said hinterlander that he'll sign for any price the producer deigns to name. And if he doesn't so deign, said hinterlander will ultimately feel so guilty about the advantage he is taking of the helpless that he'll plead for permission to sign *anything*. That he'll sign blind just to feel clean once more. The producer can fill in the figures later.

"Don't worry about price," I had been comforted by long distance. "Trust me to take care of you. I like writers. I *want* to take care of you."

It sounded fine. I had not yet felt that sun. Driving from the station, the producer's flunky assured me that the apartment I was to occupy had been vacated by a name-star only a matter of hours past. "You'll be sleeping in his bed tonight," he promised. Lucky me, I thought, that the train was late. But took the hint nonetheless that living in such a place, rent or no rent, was in itself enough to make a trip from Chicago worth any said hinterlander's while.

But didn't really feel it to be worth that much until the flunky appointed the name-star's pantry with a case of good scotch, a case of fair rye and a case of cheap bourbon; then lowered his lids to indicate we weren't to talk about money. "Don't mention it," he reassured me. I chose to mention it all the same. What I mentioned specifically was

"Where's the gin, for God's sake?" He must have thought I said "Djinn," for in only a matter of moments there appeared—precisely as in a story by John Collier[90] and all of it stuffed inside a castoff tattersall of the late Laird Cregar's[91]—a real Hollywood djinn. An honest-to-God Guru. He was fresh up from Malibu Beach and his toes stuck out of his sandals like amputated thumbs. He looked like he'd slept in a bottle with the cork in it.

It was, of course, the producer himself. And we were off to Romanoff's. I dined with him unaccompanied that first evening, a bit self-conscious of my closed-in toes. The next, I took the liberty of inviting a newfound friend. The next I took two liberties and by the time we made the Brown Derby we were blocking traffic. With my senses by now so awhirl with the wonder and hurry of it all that I had no time for gratitude.

In the faint hope of fanning some sort of spark in that direction, the djinn inquired softly, during the course of some feverish carryings-on at the Beverly-Wilshire, and the wind whisking every which way, whether I'd care to meet Miss Sylvia Sidney. The entire course of my life having been determined by the 1931 version of *An American Tragedy*, that damned near did it. That an introduction so long sought should come at a moment when my eyes weren't focusing was of no importance. Indeed, I bowed so low from the waist, in the direction I judged the lady to be, that I had just a bit of trouble straightening up. It wasn't till the following forenoon that I learned, accidentally, that

Miss Sidney was in Brussels. I felt like a sprout.

I confronted Guru with his betrayal and he didn't even redden. He was just hurt. The party to whom he'd introduced me, it turned out, was a highly effective writers' agent—so why did I have to get so salty when somebody tried to do something for me? "We'll get along better when you learn to trust others," he counseled me—and topped the bit off with the hollowest laugh I'd yet heard in The Land of Hollow Laughter.

Then he put a contract before me and confessed all: "I'm not a businessman at heart"—placing one hand over the heart to indicate precisely where he wasn't a businessman-at—"I'm just a frustrated writer."

"At heart I'm not a writer myself," I confessed in turn, placing Bernard Shaw's hand over the place where my own valentine-shaped ticker throbbed—"I'm just a frustrated businessman and I don't even trust myself."

Again in a matter of moments, but this time more as in something by Howard Fast,[92] I was evicted from the Garden of Allah where there was no Anitra near. And presented with a bill, per diem, which Guru just happened to have in his pocket. Itemizing, among other small comforts: one case of good scotch, one case of fair rye, one case of cheap bourbon. Nothing was free after all.

"Is there any relationship between my refusal to sign and my eviction?" I had just time to inquire.

He never so much as cracked. "What kind of a businessman do you think I am anyhow?" he demanded to know.

"What kind of a writer do you think I am any-how?" was all I could think to reply.

Whereupon we locked, the terrible djinn in the open-toed shoes and I in my watertight ones, in a life-and-death struggle to determine, once and for all, who was the greater jerk.

I very nearly won. I was scarcely a ranking con-tender and I was up against the champ. Smart money would have said he wouldn't even have to extend himself. Yet, on the morning he phoned to say, "After all, I *do* like you," I felt I had him.

"I like you too," I assured him. (To illustrate fur-ther the operation of affection in the Land of Hollow Laughter: while waiting in the office of a medium-size bigshot, to be introduced to a king-size bigshot, the latter entered and went directly into conference with the medi-um-size one without indicating awareness of a third party in the room except by a palm over his mouth and an occasion-al jerk of a thumb in the general direction of that party. Whispers, chuckles, thumb-jerks, a final backslap—and he had left quite as unceremoniously as he had entered. Whereupon the medium-size one assured me: "He *likes* you." And he really meant it too.)

We had reached the tacit understanding that nei-ther of us could afford anything less than affection for one another. He needed to make a million dollars and I needed to buy a house in Indiana. So though the very sight of me caused his features to be suffused by a disgust matched by nothing earthly save the revulsion in my own breast, we clung passionately each to each: a friendship based on the solid rock of utter loathing.

He showed up with a flute of Johnny Walker on one arm and a male friend on the other. By the stardust in the friend's eyes I immediately recognized an autograph-hunter. A hunter who inquired my name so shyly that I confessed, "You got me." Whereupon he put a packet of blue papers bound with a red rubber band into my hand, and the only process-server in the world with stardust-eyes excused himself.

I was alone with the Great Guru. The Great Guru from Malibu. Riffling hurriedly through the packet it became clear that he was charging me with everything from piracy on the high seas to defrauding an innkeeper. I was secretly relieved to note that he didn't have anything on me for the theft of the Stone of Scone.

"You see," he explained with that smile that succeeded so wondrously in being at once shamefaced and self-satisfied, "every time I talked long distance to you I had a lawyer on the extension."

The bird *really* liked me. Then, as if struck abruptly by the injustice of everything, he strode to the middle of the room, literally beating his breast with one hand and still clutching the bottle fiercely with the other, to turn the awful accusation upon me—"I'm a *nice* guy! Why do you make me act like a jerk?"

It wasn't the real me that made the djinn give such

an effective interpretation of a jerk. Indeed it wasn't myself at all. This impulse to do a creative job of work was genuine and pulled him hard. But the demands of the bank financing that impulse pulled him the other way, and harder. Still he stood at last with his fat toes showing, his legal threats in one hand and gifts in the other—the very personification of an industry at once predatory and propitiating. One that finds nothing untenable in going down on all fours one day crying mea culpa, promising to be a good boy and licking hands or whatever is in reach, and the next to be up and beating its breast with the terrible roar, "Movies are better than ever! Your money or your life!" A sort of kowtowing cannibalism, both abject and arrogant, sufficiently comical in either an individual clown or in a whole industry largely dominated by clowns.

Overwhelmed by what I had done to the man, I followed him about the room as hysterical as he was—"I don't know *why* I make you act like this." I broke down completely. "Everything is mixed up in my head—I don't understand myself anymore. Back home people *like* me!"

He put the bottle in my left hand and a pen that writes under water in my right.

That Yogi sun had done me in at last.

N O T E S

1. *The Crack-Up*, by F. Scott Fitzgerald, edited by Edmund Wilson (New York: New Directions, 1945), pp. 81-4. Reprinted by permission of the publisher.

2. Mark Twain to George Washington Cable, recalled by Cable at a Twain memorial reading on November 30, 1910. *Mark Twain: A Biography*, by Albert Bigelow Paine (New York: Harper & Brothers, 1912), pp. 785-6.

3. William Faulkner's address upon receiving the Nobel Prize for Literature, Stockholm, December 10, 1950. In *The Portable Faulkner*, Revised and Expanded Edition, edited by Malcolm Cowley (New York: The Viking Press, 1946, renewed 1974), pp. 723-4. Reprinted by permission of the publisher.

4. Writer-director Kazan, actor Ferrer and playwright Anderson. All were blacklisted and were among the first to testify before the House Committee on Un-American Activities (HUAC) in an attempt to clear their own names by testifying against others as former Communist Party members.

5. The Feinberg Law, enacted in New York in 1949, required teachers to report on the loyalty of their colleagues in and outside the classroom. In Illinois, the Seditions Activities Investigating Commission was created in 1947, chaired by Paul Broyles. In 1951 Broyles persuaded both houses of the Illinois legislature to pass a bill requiring state agencies to ferret out subversives. Governor Adlai Stevenson vetoed the bill. Two years later yet another Broyles bill was vetoed by the next Illinois governor, William Stratton.

6. ADA (Americans for Democratic Action), established in 1947 by establishment liberals, including Arthur Schlesinger, Jr., Reinhold Neibuhr and Hubert Humphrey. Identifying themselves as part of an intellectual elite, members of the ADA tended to be strong critics of Joe McCarthy on the one hand and fierce opponents of Henry Wallace and his Progressive Party on the other.

7. In Act Four of *Peer Gynt*, Peer is mistaken for a prophet, and in that

guise he asks his disciple and love interest Anitra, "Do you know what life consists of?... It's to be transported dry-shod down the stream of time, still unchangeably one's Self." *Peer Gynt*, by Henrik Ibsen (New York: Penguin, 1966), p. 139. See opening of Appendix.

8. Faulkner, loc. cit.

9. "Varchous" for virtuous, of course.

10. "Hypocrisy" from *Mr. Dooley on Ivrything and Ivrybody*, by Finley Patrick Dunne (New York: Dover, 1963), p. 207. Chicago-based journalist and humorist Dunne's Mr. Dooley was a fictional Irish saloonkeeper and amateur philosopher from Chicago's West Side who pondered the subtleties of current events in essays published in the *Evening Post* and *American Magazine.*

11. In the fall of 1952, the U.S. Senate Subcommittee on Privileges and Elections compiled a report on McCarthy's activities during 1948 as a member of the Senate Banking Committee and a joint committee on housing. McCarthy had accepted $10,000 from the Lustron Corporation, a builder of prefabricated houses and a regular petitioner for funds from the Reconstruction Finance Corporation (RFC), and had authored parts of the Housing Act, which included a provision allowing the RFC to make a loan of seven million dollars to Lustron in 1949. McCarthy invested the $10,000 he received from Lustron in Seaboard Airline Railroad, another company indebted to the RFC. Prompted by Senator William Benton, McCarthy's chief adversary and sponsor of a resolution calling for his expulsion, the Congressional committee labored on for a full year without managing to get McCarthy to respond to the charges. "I have not and do not intend to read, much less answer, Benton's smear attack," wrote McCarthy. The 82nd Congress ended, and McCarthy's friend William Jenner was appointed chair of the 83rd. Jenner then made the report unavailable.

12. U.S. Senator Pat McCarran of Nevada, a McCarthy supporter, was author of the International Security Act of 1950, known as the McCarran Act, which heralded a Communist conspiracy. He also co-authored the McCarran-Walter Act of 1952, which placed constraints on immigration.

13. Thorstein Veblen (1857-1929) was a prominent American economist, social philosopher and author of a number of books critiquing capitalism. In the early part of the century, American journalist Joseph Lincoln Steffens was the best-known of the muckrakers. Here Algren notes that all the old torchbearers of truth are long dead.

14. During the McCarthy era the American Legion was a proponent of blacklisting.

15. The passion and intention of this passage from Twain encapsulates

that of *The War Prayer*, which Twain dictated in 1904-5, although it is not a direct quotation. Twain's *War Prayer* bore a similar relationship to his writing career as *Nonconformity* does to Algren's. After reading it to his daughter Jean, who thought its publication would be regarded as sacrilege, and to at least one friend who clearly felt he should publish it, Twain finally decided against immediate publication: "I have told the whole truth in that," he said, "and only dead men can tell the truth in this world.... It can be published after I am dead." This famous story is told by Paine, in *Mark Twain: A Biography*.

16. Whittaker Chambers, a Communist Party member turned informer, was the first individual to testify before Dies' HUAC and name names, accusing Alger Hiss of sending secret federal documents to the Soviet Union. Hester McCullough was a Westchester (New York) housewife and amateur vigilante blacklister who became something of a right-wing *cause célèbre* when in 1950 she was sued for libel by the dancer Paul Draper and harmonica player Larry Adler.

17. From *The Spirit of Liberty: Papers and Addresses of Learned Hand, Collected and with an Introduction and Notes* by Irving Dilliard (New York: Alfred A. Knopf, 1952; Third Edition, Enlarged, 1960), p. 284. See below.

18. This passage appears towards the end of one of Learned Hand's most famous speeches. The jurist delivered the address at the convocation of the University of the State of New York in his native Albany on October 24, 1952. His words were immediately carried across the country on the news wire services, and the *Saturday Review* made the speech its feature article in the November 22, 1952, issue. Given the political climate at the time, Hand's words comprised an impassioned, if understated, plea against the status quo. See above. Reprinted by permission of the publisher.

19. Frank Yerby began his career as a writer of protest fiction, but turned to popular historical romance novels in the '40s. Emmet Kelly was a famous American circus clown. For the rest of this section, Algren scornfully refers to Yerby as "Kelly."

20. 1887 letter from Anton Chekhov to M. V. Kiseleva. From *Letters of Anton Chekhov*, Selected and edited by Avrahm Yarmolinsky (New York: The Viking Press, 1973), p. 41. Algren attacks Chekhov here under false pretenses, since Chekhov's view of the writer's responsibility closely approximated his own, and had little or nothing to do with the kind of dressed-up entertainments Algren is attacking.

21. *The Trial*, by Franz Kafka. Translated by Willa and Edwin Muir. (New York: Schocken, 1968), p. 121.

22. Fitzgerald, p. 81.

23. Hearn (1850-1904) wrote stories and essays based in the Far East; Sterling (1869-1926) was a lyric and dramatic poet.

24. André Gide's journal entry for October 8, 1891, included this observation: "This terrifies me: To think that the present, which we are living this very day, will become the mirror in which we shall later recognize ourselves; and that by what we have been we shall know what we are." *The Journals of André Gide*, Volume I: 1889-1913, Translated from the French with an introduction and notes by Justin O'Brien (New York: Alfred A. Knopf, 1947), p. 16.

25. Fleur Cowles was an editor for *Look* magazine.

26. "Books" by Joseph Conrad, a 1905 essay reprinted in *Joseph Conrad on Fiction*, edited by Walter F. Wright (Lincoln, Nebraska: University of Nebraska Press, 1964), p. 81. Reprinted by permission of the publisher.

27. Clarence Budington Kelland was an author of juvenile novels and editor of *The American Boy*.

28. Algren seems to have taken this passage from an English language edition of *The Illuminations* available at the time he was writing, and then perhaps condensed it—or he was quoting from memory. The Louise Varèse translation of this passage differs substantially: "The poet makes himself a *visionary* through a long, a prodigious and rational disordering of *all* the senses. Every form of love, of suffering, of madness; he searches himself, he consumes all the poisons in him, keeping only their quintessences. Ineffable torture in which he will need all his faith and superhuman strength, the great criminal, the great sick-man, the accursed,—and the supreme Savant! For he arrives at the unknown! Since he has cultivated his soul—richer to begin with than any other! He arrives at the unknown: and even if, half crazed, in the end, he loses the understanding of his visions, he has seen them!" From an 1871 letter from Arthur Rimbaud to Paul Demeny, printed as a preface to *The Illuminations,* by Arthur Rimbaud, translated by Louise Varèse (New York: New Directions, 1946), pp. xxx-xxxi.

29. Popular 1940s novels by Frank Yerby and Louis Bromfield, respectively.

30. Conrad, pp. 81-2.

31. The *Saturday Evening Blade* was a Chicago tabloid newspaper, hawked by Algren in his boyhood. See Algren's "Merry Christmas Mr. Mark" in *The Last Carousel*, pp. 293-4.

32. "Our April Letter" in "The Note-Books" in Fitzgerald, p. 165.

33. Fitzgerald, p. 81.

34. Booth Tarkington was an American novelist and short story writer, author of dozens of books, including *The Magnificent Ambersons* and *Alice Adams*, both winners of the Pulitzer Prize.

35. Fitzgerald, p. 84.

36. Ibid., p. 80-3.

37. In his autobiography, *Nice Guys Finish Last* (New York: Simon and Schuster, 1975, pp. 13, 15 and 26), Durocher gives substantially the same account and adds that in his early years his mother read his words in a newspaper and gave him hell. Algren probably got his version from the same newspaper story as Durocher's mother.

38. *Notes from Underground* by Fyodor Dostoevsky. In *Dostoevsky: Notes from Underground, White Nights, The Dream of a Ridiculous Man* and *Selections from The House of the Dead* translated by Andrew R. MacAndrew (New York: New American Library, 1980), p. 129.

39. Soon after completing *Nonconformity*, Algren would begin his most ambitious novel ever, with a plot line that turns on characters closely linked to those invoked here. Called *Entrapment*, it tells the story of Baby, a country woman turned prostitute (modeled after Algren's very close friend, a prostitute named Margo), and Daddy, her heroin-using husband. When Daddy gets busted, Baby robs from her tricks to get him out of jail. Algren never finished the book, although there exist several hundred manuscript pages.

40. *The Diary of a Writer*, by F. M. Dostoevsky, translated and annotated by Boris Brasol. (New York: George Braziller, 1954), p. 7. Reprinted by permission of the publisher. Algren has chosen a passage early in *Diary of a Writer* in which Dostoevsky is actually quoting the Russian literary critic Belinsky. The section from which the passage is taken deals not only with the misery of those excluded from mainstream society, but goes on to discuss Dostoevsky's near execution and four years of hard labor, which he later described as vitally important to his development as a writer, where his enforced contact with other convicts gave him knowledge of the Russian lower classes possessed by no other contemporary Russian author. See below.

41. *The Second Sex*, by Simone de Beauvoir. Translated and edited by H. M. Parshley. (New York: Alfred A. Knopf, Inc., 1952, renewed 1980. Vintage Books Edition, 1989), p. 713.

As noted by Algren's biographer Bettina Drew, in the summer of 1953—which began with the June executions of Julius and Ethel Rosenberg, which horrified Algren, and while he still waited to hear from Doubleday on the publication plans for this essay—Algren claimed he read all 750 pages of de Beauvoir's magnum opus. De Beauvoir, though still deeply bound to Algren, had by now distanced herself from him sufficiently to be deeply at work on *The Mandarins*, the novel that would recreate their love affair, and to have taken on a new lover in the future documentary filmmaker Claude *(Shoah)* Lanzmann. But Algren was still deeply in love with de Beauvoir, even though more than a year had passed since he'd seen her, a period during which he'd reconciled with his first wife Amanda. And just as missing Simone must have been part of the experience of reading *The Second Sex,* so writing *Nonconformity* was also in part an attempt to prove to her that he was as worthy of her as Sartre was. The passage in question precedes by a few pages the conclusion to *The Second Sex* and comes as part of an argument whose polemical thrust is that, as she writes, "to explain her limitations it is woman's situation that must be invoked and not a mysterious essence." Both Algren and de Beauvoir extend the analogy beyond the specific context—from the condition of women to that of blacks, the French proletariat or the American underclass. See Afterword. Reprinted by permission of the publisher.

42. Dostoevsky, *Diary of a Writer,* p. 16. At the peak of his career, during the period of his last years that produced *The Possessed* and *The Brothers Karamazov,* Dostoevsky also produced this huge and unwieldy work of autobiographical journalism pieced together from a variety of sources in the form of a diary. Informal and colloquial in tone, dealing in large part with political questions of the day, the work has been compared to Rousseau's *Confessions* or Goethe's *Poetry and Truth.* See above.

43. *America Day by Day,* by Simone de Beauvoir. Translated by Patrick Dudley (pseud.). (New York: Grove Press, 1953), p. 294.

44. The phrase sounds distinctly like one of Algren's, and indeed he is paraphrasing and condensing de Beauvoir here so freely that he has rewritten her, perhaps without fully realizing it. To have restored her wording in this case would have been to change his meaning.

Here is a passage from the conclusion of *America Day by Day,* de Beauvoir's account of her four-month trip across America in 1947 in which she first met Algren, which may have been the source for Algren's sentence: "There are very few ambitious people here.... Ambitions for greatness are often the source of many deceptions, and indicted by faults Americans do not know; they have virtues born of indifference to themselves. They are not embittered, persecuted or ill-willed, envious or egotistical. But they have no inner fire. In order to lose themselves in the pursuit of an object, they find themselves without an object at all." p. 294.

45. Letter from Anton Chekhov to A. S. Suvorin, written from Nice on February 6, 1898. In *Letters of Anton Chekhov,* selected and edited by Avrahm Yarmolinsky, translated by Bernard Guilbert Guerney and Lynn Solotaroff. (New York: The Viking Press, 1973), p. 304. The reference here is to the Dreyfus case. Chekhov's letter was written from France on the eve of the trial of Zola for his exposé *(J'accuse!)* of the court-martial that acquitted Major Esterhazy in the Dreyfus case. Chekhov passionately

supported Zola's stand against the hypocrisy of the attack on Dreyfus and argued it repeatedly in letters to his friend and publisher Suvorin. The same letter that Algren quotes, for example, begins, "You write that you are vexed by Zola, but here [Nice] the general feeling is as if a new, better Zola has been born. In this trial of his he has been cleansed of superficial grease spots as by turpentine, and shines forth before the French in his true splendor. It is a purity, a moral loftiness that no one suspected."

46. Fulton Sheen, a Roman Catholic Bishop of New York, was a noted radio and TV preacher who won the 1952 Emmy as most outstanding male personality on television. Fulton Oursler was a writer and editor on religious themes, author of *The Greatest Story Ever Told*. Fulton Lewis was a radio commentator.

47. *America Day by Day*, by de Beauvoir, pp. 80-1. This account of de Beauvoir's first evening with Algren was not, as is self-evident, part of Algren's original essay. I include it here to maintain the consistency of the structure of Algren's essay, in which he alternated his own words with long quotes from other writers, and as a rare window into Algren's sensibility since, as in this essay itself, it shows Algren, uncharacteristically, revealing the sources of his inspiration. Reprinted by permission of the publisher.

48. Popular singer of the period, whose number one hit was called "Cry."

49. Mafia bosses.

50. Hawkins and Young were jazz tenor saxophonists; the Mills Brothers are credited with founding the "black-harmony" singing style and paving the way for 50s rock and roll; the Billy Williams Quartet performed weekly on Ceasar & Coca's "Your Show of Shows" in the 1950s; singers in the "hep harmony" tradition, Monroe and Laine were singers of, respectively, the 1930s and 40s; Gene Krupa was a "Chicago style" jazz drummer, while Jackie Cooper, an actor, possibly made it to this list for the poetic similarity of his name to Krupa's; or perhaps Algren mistakenly thought Cooper had played Krupa in the biopic *The Gene Krupa Story*.

51. The Bridewell Cure was a cold turkey "cure" named after the Illinois prison where the practice was notorious.

52. *Conversations with Nelson Algren*, by H. E. F. Donohue (New York: Hill and Wang, 1964), pp. 279-80.

53. Letter from Chekhov to A. S. Suvorin, February 6, 1898. In Chekhov, p. 305.

54. Westbrook Pegler was a newspaper columnist known for attacks on corruption in politics and on labor unions.

55. Kafka, p. 228. This passage is from the second-to-last paragraph of the novel, which concludes with K. declining to do himself in, and then losing his life anyway, at the hands of his two executioners, "like a dog."

Reprinted by permission of the publisher.

56. *New Testament*, Romans 7:19. The King James version reads, "For the good that I would, I do not: but the evil which I would not, that I do." *The New English Bible* version reads, "The good which I want to do, I fail to do; but what I do is the wrong which is against my will."

57. *Alice in Justice-Land: From Pippins and Cheese*, by Jake Falstaff, published as a column in *The New York World* in the summer of 1929 and subsequently reprinted by the American Civil Liberties Union (New York: ACLU Publications, 1935).

58. Kafka, pp. 45-6.

59. Ibid., pp 228-9.

60. As U.S. Secretary of State from 1953 to 1959, John Foster Dulles emphasized "collective security" in foreign policy and the concept of a strong national defense capable of immediate retaliation as a deterrent to war.

61. *Democratic Vistas*, by Walt Whitman. Washington, D.C., 1871, pp. 11-12. As reprinted in *The Portable Walt Whitman*, edited by Mark van Doren, revised by Malcolm Cowley. (New York: Penguin, 1945, 1973), pp. 325-26. Algren's *Nonconformity* is about the same length—pamphlet length—as Whitman's *Democratic Vistas* and both embody the same broadsheet-like populist passion, both exhibit the same spirit of restlessness and impatience and both seem to allow themselves only reluctantly, almost petulantly, to be formed as essays, rather than, say, shouts from a Union Square or Madison Square soapbox. So *Democratic Vistas* is a most important antecedent for Algren in writing *Nonconformity*. In both, we are seeing writers unburden themselves of the harsh beliefs and perceptions that would usually go unsaid, and by so doing close, or move beyond, an earlier period of extraordinary fecundity—that had produced *Leaves of Grass* for Whitman, and in Algren's case the period, just ended, that had produced *Neon Wilderness, Never Come Morning, Chicago: City on the Make* and *The Man with the Golden Arm*.

62. "Murther" for murder, of course.

63. Whitman, loc. cit.

NOTES TO AFTERWORD:

64. Letter from Algren to Joseph Haas, March 1, 1952. Quoted in *Nelson Algren: A Life on the Wild Side,* by Bettina Drew, (New York: G. P. Putnam's Sons, 1989), p. 198.

65. "Nelson Algren," *Paris Review* 11 (Winter 1955) by Alston Anderson and Terry Southern, pp. 39-40. Reprinted in *Writers at Work: The Paris*

Review Interviews, edited by Malcolm Cowley (New York: The Viking Press, 1959), p. 234.

"I'd spent almost two years on the book before I ever ran into a drug addict," Algren adds a little later in the interview; "I had the book written about a card-dealer, but there wasn't any dope angle at all.... It was an afterthought." And further on, speaking of his writing method generally: "I've always figured the only way I could finish a book and get a plot was just to keep making it longer and longer until something happens— you know, until it finds its own plot.... I suppose it's a slow way of working." (Ibid., pp. 236, 238, 240.)

66. Donohue, p. 101.

67. Besides the aforementioned Geismar, these include Algren's contemporary George Bluestone and our contemporaries Tom Carson and James R. Giles.

68. Nelson Algren quoted in *Daily Worker,* March 3, 1952, p. 3.

69. Donohue, p. 73

70. Introduction by Tom Carson, in *The Neon Wilderness: Stories by Nelson Algren* (New York: Seven Stories Press, 1986). Adapted from an essay originally published in the *Village Voice.*

71. Donohue, p. 163.

72. *Never Come Morning,* by Nelson Algren (New York: Harper Colophon Books, 1941, 1942, 1963), p. xiii.

73 This account is based on the description of the genesis of *Never Come Morning* in Drew, pp. 134-5.

74. *Confronting the Horror: The Novels of Nelson Algren,* by James R. Giles (Kent, Ohio: The Kent State University Press, 1989).

75. Drew, p. 197.

76. See Giles, p. 6.

77. Donohue, pp. 158, 160-61.

78. The two sentences dictated, signed and dated by Algren are attached to Bradley's memorandum, along with the following handwritten note signed by Bradley: "I wrote the above notation in Nelson's presence and at his dictation, whereupon he signed it." Courtesy of the Ohio University Libraries.

79. From a memorandum by Van Allen Bradley on *Chicago Daily News* stationery dated January 2, 1960, which Bradley attached to the carbon of Algren's essay. Courtesy of the Ohio University Libraries.

80. *Nelson Algren: A Descriptive Bibliography,* by Matthew J. Bruccoli with the assistance of Judith Baughman (Pittsburgh: University of Pittsburgh Press, 1985), pp. 112-13.

81. *The Nation* published their excerpt as "American Christmas, 1952" in the December 27 issue that year, another sample that summer as "Hollywood Djinn with a Dash of Bitters" (25 July 1953) and another version in the October 17, 1953, issue under the title "Eggheads Are Rolling: The Rush to Conform."

82. The quotes and historical account in this and the preceding paragraph are drawn from Bradley's prefatory note, which he appended to the carbon, presumably when he delivered it into the Algren Archive. Courtesy of the Ohio University Libraries.

Bradley's account may not be perfectly factual, in that the essay and the lecture seem to have been roughly identical from the start, and may have existed prior to Bradley's request that Algren contribute something to the Christmas book section of the *Chicago Daily News*.

83. Drew, pp. 244-45.

84. Drew, pp. 245-46.

85. Drew, p. 252.

86. Ibid.

87. From *Mark Twain: A Biography*, by Albert Bigelow Paine (New York: Harper & Brothers, 1912). Reprinted in *The War Prayer*, by Mark Twain with drawings by John Groth (New York: Harper Colophon Books, 1970), *frontis.*

88. Bradley probably wrote his explanatory memorandum, dated January 2, 1960, as part of the preparations for placing these documents with the archive.

NOTES TO APPENDIX:

89. The Garden of Allah bungalow court and hotel was a famed and fashionable residence of writers in the film industry, including F. Scott Fitzgerald and Robert Benchley. Situated on Sunset Boulevard at Crescent Heights in Hollywood, it was razed in 1960.

90. John Collier, a British-born American writer, was best known for satiric and grotesque fiction including *His Monkey Wife* (1930, a novel) and *Fancies and Goodnights* (1951, short stories).

91. Laird Cregar was a Hollywood actor who died in 1944.

92. Howard Fast, an American novelist and story writer, espoused activist politics in books like *Citizen Tom Paine* (1943) and *Freedom Road* (1944). He later abandoned the Communist Party, revealing in *The Naked God* (1957) his bitterness with it.